How
OJJDP Is
Forming
Partnerships
and Finding Solutions

ANNUAL REPORT

This report covers activities undertaken by the Office of Juvenile Justice and Delinquency Prevention during fiscal year 2010 (October 1, 2009–September 30, 2010)

NCJ 237051

U.S. Department of Justice
Office of Justice Programs
810 Seventh Street NW.
Washington, DC 20531

Eric H. Holder, Jr.
Attorney General

Mary Lou Leary
Acting Assistant Attorney General

Melodee Hanes
Acting Administrator
Office of Juvenile Justice and Delinquency Prevention

Office of Justice Programs
Innovation • Partnerships • Safer Neighborhoods
www.ojp.usdoj.gov

Office of Juvenile Justice and Delinquency Prevention
www.ojjdp.gov

The Office of Juvenile Justice and Delinquency Prevention is a component of the Office of Justice Programs, which also includes the Bureau of Justice Assistance; the Bureau of Justice Statistics; the National Institute of Justice; the Office for Victims of Crime; and the Office of Sex Offender Sentencing, Monitoring, Apprehending, Registering, and Tracking.

To the President, the Attorney General, the President pro tempore of the Senate, the Speaker of the House of Representatives, the Chairmen of the Committees on the Judiciary of the Senate and the House of Representatives, the Chairman of the Committee on Education and the Workforce of the House of Representatives, and Members of Congress

It is my honor to transmit the Office of Juvenile Justice and Delinquency Prevention's (OJJDP's) annual report for fiscal year 2010. This report includes information pursuant to:

- OJJDP Annual Report—Juvenile Justice and Delinquency Prevention (JJDP) Act of 1974, as amended; Public Law 93–415, section 207 [42 U.S.C. 5617].

- Missing Children Program—JJDP Act of 1974, as amended; Public Law 93–415, section 404(a)(5) [42 U.S.C. 5773(a)(5)].

- Juvenile Accountability Block Grants Program—Omnibus Crime Control and Safe Streets Act of 1968; Public Law 90–351, section 1808(b) [42 U.S.C. 3796ee–8(b)].

- Title V—JJDP Act of 1974, as amended; Public Law 93–415, section 503(4) [42 U.S.C. 5782(4)].

- Boys & Girls Clubs in Public Housing Projects—Economic Espionage Act of 1996; Public Law 104–294, section 401(d) [42 U.S.C. 13751 note].

Respectfully submitted,

Melodee Hanes
Acting Administrator
Office of Juvenile Justice and Delinquency Prevention
Washington, DC

FOREWORD

We are pleased to present the Office of Juvenile Justice and Delinquency Prevention's (OJJDP's) fiscal year (FY) 2010 Annual Report.

As this report describes, OJJDP remains steadfastly committed to evidence-based approaches for preventing and intervening in delinquency. At the same time, the Office works every day to protect innocent children from abuse, exploitation, abduction, and violence. We know all too well that youth who have experienced repeated violence and trauma suffer many possible adverse consequences, including depression, substance abuse, dropping out of school, and a drift into delinquent behavior.

During FY 2010, OJJDP played an important role in the Attorney General's Defending Childhood initiative. The goals of the initiative include preventing children's exposure to violence in their families and communities, mitigating the effects of this violence on children, and raising awareness of the problem. OJJDP's groundbreaking research on children's exposure to violence serves as the underpinning of the Defending Childhood initiative. These research findings include the disturbing truth that more than 60 percent of the nation's youth have been exposed to violence, crime, or abuse within the past year, either directly or indirectly.

In FY 2010, OJJDP awarded more than $519 million in grants in support of its mission to address juvenile delinquency and child victimization. This amount included more than $96 million through mentoring appropriations to support programs across the country that are improving youth's self-esteem and academic achievement and encouraging them to move ahead to a successful future.

Using information gleaned from OJJDP research on the risk and protective factors specific to girls, we launched the National Girls Institute, which serves as the first national clearinghouse of information for at-risk and justice-system-involved girls, their families, and service providers. It also offers the training and technical assistance that is so urgently needed by those who work in the area of gender-specific programming.

As part of our ongoing effort to leverage resources with our partners in the private sector, OJJDP joined with the Annie E. Casey Foundation to fund an expansion of the Juvenile Detention Alternatives Initiative, which aims (among other objectives) to eliminate the inappropriate or unnecessary use of secure detention for youth and redirect public finances to sustain successful reform in the juvenile justice system.

These are only a few examples of the work OJJDP is doing to help make our communities safer places to live, to keep the juvenile justice field informed of the latest developments in research, and to give children who are at risk or who are involved in the justice system an opportunity to lead healthy and productive lives. I am excited about the opportunity to build on these achievements in the months and years ahead.

Melodee Hanes
Acting Administrator
Office of Juvenile Justice and Delinquency Prevention

ABOUT OJJDP

The Office of Juvenile Justice and Delinquency Prevention (OJJDP) was established by Congress through the Juvenile Justice and Delinquency Prevention (JJDP) Act of 1974, Public Law 93–415, as amended. A component of the Office of Justice Programs within the U.S. Department of Justice, OJJDP works to prevent and control juvenile delinquency, improve the juvenile justice system, and protect children.

Mission Statement

OJJDP provides national leadership, coordination, and the resources to prevent and respond to juvenile delinquency and victimization. OJJDP supports states and communities in their efforts to develop and implement effective and coordinated prevention and intervention programs and to improve the juvenile justice system so that it protects public safety, holds offenders accountable, and provides treatment and rehabilitative services tailored to the needs of juveniles and their families.

Organization

OJJDP is composed of the Office of the Administrator, three program divisions (Child Protection, Demonstration Programs, and State Relations and Assistance), the Office of Policy Development (including the Communications Unit), and the Grants Management Unit. Appendix C summarizes each component's role.

TABLE OF CONTENTS

CHAPTER 1

CHAPTER 1

OJJDP Is
Forming Partnerships and Finding Solutions: Major Accomplishments

Over the past decade, the Office of Juvenile Justice and Delinquency Prevention (OJJDP) has made great strides in bringing together federal, state, local, and tribal agencies; communities; and components of the juvenile justice system to address youth crime and victimization. Collaboration characterized many of OJJDP's activities in fiscal year (FY) 2010, including programs to address issues related to gang and community violence, offender reentry, and missing and exploited children.

Programs must stand up to rigorous evaluation and examination to prove their merit. OJJDP sets a high priority on funding activities and programs that have a solid record of success. This means supporting evidence-based programs that reduce juvenile delinquency and crime, protect children from sexual exploitation and abuse, and improve the juvenile justice system.

The Office's many accomplishments in FY 2010 included helping the field understand and address pressing issues such as the prevalence of Internet crimes against youth, the need for prevention and intervention programs that meet the specific needs of at-risk and delinquent girls, and the long-term negative consequences of children's exposure to violence. The activities highlighted in this chapter and throughout the report illustrate OJJDP's ongoing commitment to finding solutions that have the greatest potential for improving the juvenile justice system and keeping communities safe.

To make the best use of public resources, OJJDP is committed to identifying "what works" in delinquency prevention and juvenile justice. OJJDP has partnered with many federal agencies to find solutions that have the greatest potential for improving the juvenile justice system and keeping communities safe.

In FY 2010, OJJDP awarded more than $915 million in grants in support of its mission to prevent and respond to juvenile delinquency and child victimization, including nearly $389 million in discretionary funding. Detailed information about these awards is available in appendix A.

Evidence-Based Practices

OJJDP has a long history of promoting evidence-based programs and practices. In 2000, the Office established the Model Programs Guide (MPG), one of the first comprehensive resources to identify evidence-based programs in juvenile justice and delinquency prevention. It has since evolved into an online resource with a variety of specialized databases. The MPG, which currently includes 200 evidence-based programs, is designed to assist practitioners and communities in implementing prevention and intervention programs that can make a difference in the lives of children and communities. The MPG's growing database of programs covers the continuum of youth services, from prevention through sanctions to reentry.

Building on these efforts, in FY 2010 the Office of Justice Programs (OJP) began developing CrimeSolutions.gov, a comprehensive online resource that uses rigorous evaluation evidence to assess program effectiveness across a broad range of juvenile and adult criminal justice and victims' programs. The online tool is part of OJP's Evidence Integration Initiative, which seeks to improve the quantity and quality of evidence that OJP generates through research, evaluation, and statistics; to better integrate evidence into program and policy decisions; and to improve the translation of evidence into practice. The initiative established teams within OJP to synthesize evidence on specific justice topics and develop principles for practice that can be communicated to the field. Over the next several years, OJJDP will complete the process of aligning the MPG's review standards and evidence ratings with those of CrimeSolutions.gov to ensure conformity between the two sites.

For more information on OJJDP's Model Programs Guide, see chapter 3.

Children's Exposure to Violence

Children's exposure to violence—whether as a victim or as a witness—is associated with long-term physical, psychological, and emotional harm. These children are at higher risk of mental health problems such as anxiety and depression. They are also more likely to use drugs and alcohol, and even to engage in violent behavior themselves.

Launched in FY 2010, Attorney General Eric Holder's Defending Childhood initiative directs resources for the express purpose of reducing children's exposure to violence, raising awareness of its ramifications, and advancing scientific inquiry on its causes and characteristics. At the Department of Justice (DOJ), offices covering a broad range of issues—from violence against women and juvenile justice to community-based policing and victims of crime—are actively engaged in coordinating efforts to prevent children's exposure to violence. The initiative also involves partnerships with the U.S. Departments of Education and Health and Human Services, as well as with law enforcement and U.S. Attorneys' Offices across the country.

For more than 10 years, OJJDP has been a national leader in addressing this critical issue. Under the leadership of then Deputy Attorney General Holder in June 1999, OJJDP launched the Safe Start initiative to broaden knowledge about and promote community investment in evidence-based strategies for reducing the impact of children's exposure to violence. The Defending Childhood initiative is building on the foundation established by Safe Start to expand partnerships among family- and youth-serving agencies such as early childhood education/ development, health, mental health, child welfare, family support, substance abuse prevention/intervention, domestic violence/crisis intervention, law enforcement, the courts, and legal services.

For more information on the Defending Childhood initiative, see chapter 4.

Girls' Delinquency

Rising trends in girls' delinquency in the 1990s led OJJDP to call for more gender-related research on delinquency prevention and intervention. To address this need and provide comprehensive information on female delinquency, the Office created its Girls Study Group in 2004. Several other OJJDP-sponsored programs also have undertaken efforts to enhance the juvenile justice system's response to girls' delinquency. The Office provides training and technical assistance, gender-specific programming, assessment tools, publications, and other resources.

One highlight of FY 2010 was OJJDP's award of a $1.5-million, 3-year grant to the Center for Girls and Young Women at the National Council on Crime and Delinquency to establish the National Girls Institute (NGI). The Institute will provide training and technical assistance to programs that address the needs of girls who are at risk or who are involved in the juvenile justice system. NGI will also disseminate information; collaborate with researchers and program developers; form partnerships with federal, state, tribal, and local agencies; and develop policy.

OJJDP also awarded grants to researchers at the Development Services Group, the University of Virginia, and the University of Connecticut to evaluate juvenile delinquency prevention, intervention, and treatment programs, which traditionally have been designed with boys in mind, to determine how well girls respond to these interventions.

In addition, the Girls Study Group conducted an Evaluation Technical Assistance Workshop in Chapel Hill, NC, to equip select organizations with the resources they need to carry out rigorous evaluations of their gender-responsive delinquency prevention and intervention programs, which are designed specifically to meet the unique needs of girls.

More information about FY 2010 Girls Study Group publications may be found in chapter 5.

Anti-Gang Initiatives

In the 1970s, fewer than half of the states reported gang problems. However, by the turn of the 21st century, every state and the District of Columbia were facing this challenge. Recognizing that youth gangs are a serious national issue, OJJDP supports the development and implementation of demonstration programs that address gang prevention, intervention, and suppression, as well as gang-related research and evaluation activities, training and technical assistance, and information dissemination.

In FY 2010, OJJDP completed work on the second edition of *Best Practices To Address Community Gang Problems: OJJDP's Comprehensive Gang Model*, a publication that provides guidance on how communities can best address an existing or emerging youth gang problem. The report, released in October 2009, describes the research that produced OJJDP's Comprehensive Gang Model and offers best practices obtained from practitioners with years of experience in planning, implementing, and overseeing variations of the model within their communities. The second edition includes a summary of findings from an independent evaluation of OJJDP's Gang Reduction Program, a demonstration of the anti-gang framework in four target sites.

OJJDP's anti-gang activities are described in more detail in chapter 2.

Mentoring

Mentoring helps prevent at-risk youth from becoming involved in delinquency and also helps delinquent youth change their lives for the better. Mentoring relationships have been shown to improve youth's self-esteem, behavior, and academic performance. OJJDP has long supported mentoring as an effective way to prevent at-risk youth from becoming involved in delinquency.

In FY 2010, OJJDP continued its significant investment in mentoring programs. The Office funded juvenile mentoring grants to support national and community organizations that directly serve youth through mentoring, target specific populations of youth, and enhance the capacity of other organizations to recruit, train, and supervise mentors.

A priority of the Office is the development of evidence-based practices for mentoring. In FY 2010, OJJDP's new Mentoring Research Best Practices Program was launched to identify the specific components of mentoring programs that have a significant impact in reducing juvenile delinquency and offending.

OJJDP's many mentoring initiatives are described in detail in chapter 2.

OJJDP AD CAMPAIGN URGES PROSPECTIVE MENTORS TO STEP UP TO THE PLATE

In FY 2010, OJJDP continued its Be a Mentor campaign. OJJDP reached some 3.5 million people through its ad in the game programs for Major League Baseball's 2010 American League and National League Championship Series and the World Series. The ad, which invites adults to "step up to the plate" by becoming a mentor, also appeared in the program for the 2011 All-Star game.

Juvenile Reentry

The Second Chance Act of 2007 provides a comprehensive response to the increasing number of people who are released from prison, jail, and juvenile residential facilities and are returning to their communities. There are more than 81,000 youth in residential confinement within the juvenile justice system on any given day. The vast majority of these youth will eventually be released and will return to their communities.

OJJDP and the Office of Justice Programs' Bureau of Justice Assistance (BJA) are collaborating closely on the implementation of the Second Chance Act to ensure that both juvenile and adult reentry efforts are provided with the funding and resources to effectively reduce recidivism, protect public safety, and return offenders successfully to their communities. In FY 2010, OJJDP funding focused on implementing indepth assessments that identify offenders at high risk of recidivism, providing a comprehensive range of services for offenders, and ensuring sustained case planning and management.

Reentry provides a major opportunity to reduce recidivism, save taxpayer dollars, and make our communities safer. . . . By developing effective, evidence-based reentry programs, we can improve public safety and community well-being.

—Attorney General Eric Holder

Bullying Prevention

The harmful effects of bullying cannot be overstated. Reports of bullying in the 1990s show that, in extreme cases, victims may face shooting or severe beatings and may even turn to suicide. These reports have triggered public action, prompting more than 20 states to enact laws requiring that schools provide education and services directed toward the prevention and cessation of bullying.

To determine the causes of bullying in schools and to inform the development of effective intervention strategies, OJJDP funded a series of studies in 2007 at the National Center for School Engagement (NCSE). The research focused on the connection between different types and frequencies of bullying and truancy and student achievement, and whether students' engagement in school mediates these factors. In FY 2010, OJJDP started work on a new publication series that summarizes findings from NCSE's research. To learn more about the publication series, see chapter 5.

OJJDP represented DOJ on the Federal Partners interagency workgroup that sponsored the first Federal Partners in Bullying Prevention Summit, held in Washington, DC, in August 2010. The summit was organized by the U.S. Departments of Education, Justice, Health and Human Services, Defense, Agriculture, and the Interior; and the Centers for Disease Control and Prevention.

The summit brought together professionals involved in helping to prevent and reduce bullying and cyberbullying in schools and communities across the country. Researchers, practitioners, federal officials, members of faith-based organizations, and youth attended. Speakers included Arne Duncan, Secretary of the Department of Education; Tom Perrelli, Associate Attorney General; and Dr. Regina M. Benjamin, Surgeon General of the United States.

OJJDP sponsored a followup Webinar in October to enable summit participants and other professionals in the field to recapture the information shared at the summit and to expand their knowledge on how to effectively deal with issues associated with bullying and cyberbullying.

Youth in Custody

Staff in juvenile detention and confinement facilities need high-quality training and technical assistance to ensure that they provide for the safety, security, and rehabilitation of youth in their custody.

In 2010, OJJDP responded to the field-generated call for assistance, leadership, and support to improve conditions in youth and adult facilities housing juvenile offenders[1] by creating the National Center for Youth in Custody. The Council of Juvenile Correctional Administrators and the National Partnership for Juvenile Services codirect the center.

---

[1] These may include juvenile correctional, juvenile detention, and court-holding facilities; group homes; and adult prisons, jails, and lockups.

The center has three priorities: to help those who work with youth in custody improve the conditions of custody and confinement for youth; to support and enhance compliance with the four core protections of the Juvenile Justice and Delinquency Prevention Act; and to strengthen family and community engagement in all aspects of youth custody. The center offers a resource library, training and training curriculums, Webinars, professional development planning, and technical assistance.

Indigent Defense

More than 40 years have passed since the landmark Supreme Court decisions in *Gideon* v. *Wainwright* and *In re Gault,* which established the right to counsel for adults and juveniles in criminal and delinquency cases, respectively. Despite the decades that have elapsed since the Court's decisions, these cases have yet to be fully translated into reality. In too many counties and communities, too many people—including juveniles—may never have a lawyer.

As a means of highlighting and addressing this important issue, approximately 500 public defenders, prosecutors, judges, legislators, government officials, and representatives from leading advocacy organizations gathered in February 2010 for the National Symposium on Indigent Defense in Washington, DC. Sponsored by DOJ with the support of OJJDP and BJA, the symposium encompassed 5 plenary sessions and more than 40 workshops related to indigent adult and juvenile defense. Senior officials and staff from OJJDP served as moderators for numerous workshop discussions on strategies to enhance juvenile defense.

In addition, in FY 2010 OJJDP funded the creation of a national clearinghouse for juvenile defense attorneys to provide publications and resources, information about policy development and leadership opportunities, and training and technical assistance on indigent defense issues. This clearinghouse will improve the overall level of systemic advocacy, enhance the quality of juvenile indigent defense representation, and ensure professional and ongoing technical support to the juvenile indigent defense bar.

Interagency Partnerships To Address Key Youth Issues

Chaired by Attorney General Eric Holder and administered by OJJDP, the Coordinating Council on Juvenile Justice and Delinquency Prevention charted the course for future interagency collaboration in FY 2010 by identifying four priority issues for consideration and action: education and at-risk youth, tribal youth and juvenile justice, juvenile reentry and transition to adulthood, and racial

and/or ethnic disparities in the juvenile justice system and related systems. The list of priorities was the culmination of extensive consultations between OJJDP, DOJ staff, and officials from the Council's 13 member agencies and 4 affiliate federal members.

Multidisciplinary teams staffed by the Council's member agencies are developing recommendations to the President and to Congress for enhancing federal practice in these priority areas. The recommendations will be based on indepth analyses of policies, legislation, budgets, regulations, and practices that foster as well as hinder effective collaboration between federal, state, and local partners.

"For us at the Justice Department, I consider the work of this Council as a legacy," said Attorney General Holder at the January 2010 meeting at which the Council approved the four priority areas. "This is something I hope our Justice Department will be remembered for . . . a time when the Council came up with real solutions to real problems."

COORDINATING COUNCIL ON JUVENILE JUSTICE AND DELINQUENCY PREVENTION

The Coordinating Council on Juvenile Justice and Delinquency Prevention is an independent body within the executive branch of the federal government and it operates under the Federal Advisory Committee Act of 1972. The Council is dedicated to fostering multisector partnerships to improve the policies and practices of federal, state, and local programs for youth.

The Council is made up of 22 members—13 *ex officio* and affiliate members and 9 practitioners. The *ex officio* members are: the Attorney General; the Administrator of the Office of Juvenile Justice and Delinquency Prevention; the Secretaries of the U.S. Departments of Education, Health and Human Services (HHS), Housing and Urban Development, and Labor; the Assistant Secretary of Immigration and Customs Enforcement in the U.S. Department of Homeland Security; the Director of the Office of National Drug Control Policy; and the Chief Executive Officer of the Corporation for National and Community Service. Affiliate members are the Secretaries of the U.S. Departments of Agriculture, Defense, and the Interior, and the Administrator of the Substance Abuse and Mental Health Services Administration of HHS. The nine juvenile justice practitioner members are appointed by the Speaker of the House of Representatives, the Senate Majority Leader, and the President of the United States.

Emergency Planning for Juvenile Justice Residential Facilities

During FY 2010, OJJDP partnered with the National Commission on Children and Disasters to explore creative ways to support state planning activities pertaining to disaster preparedness of youth-serving systems across the nation. OJJDP leads the Justice Working Group on Children and Disasters, which is composed of experts in emergency preparedness, juvenile justice, health and human services, the courts, and education.

The group worked to develop a guidance document, *Emergency Planning for Juvenile Justice Residential Facilities,* that will assist decisionmakers in developing plans to ensure the safety and well-being of youth in custody in the event of a disaster. The document addresses a range of issues, including information sharing across agencies, alternate locations for housing youth, evacuation procedures, emergency staffing of juvenile justice facilities, communication, and mental health services. The document was released at OJJDP's National Conference in October 2011.

Listening Sessions

OJJDP is communicating with its partners in the juvenile justice field on challenges and solutions through regularly scheduled listening sessions. These interactive sessions, launched in May 2009, foster an ongoing dialog with policymakers and practitioners on the current trends and issues facing the juvenile justice field. The sessions enhance OJJDP's collective knowledge base, help guide decisionmaking and planning, and promote open and transparent governing. Topics addressed in past sessions include child protection, research and evaluation, reducing disproportionate minority contact, and trends in the juvenile justice system.

In February 2010, OJJDP officials and staff along with representatives of other OJP components met with training and technical assistance experts in Washington, DC, to discuss trends and challenges in the field. Participants identified major trends, including the need for evidence-based practices, strategies to address the problem of disproportionate minority contact within the juvenile justice system, and gender-responsive mental health services. Major challenges cited were the marketing of training and technical assistance services to rural and tribal areas, many of which do not have Internet access; high staff turnover; the need to provide culturally appropriate services; and the need for national training and technical assistance standards.

CHAPTER 2

OJJDP Is
Working To Prevent and Intervene in Delinquency

CHAPTER 2

For delinquency prevention efforts to be successful, they must be coordinated at the local, tribal, state, and federal levels with law enforcement, social services, child welfare, public health, mental health, school, and other systems that address family strengthening and youth development. This collaborative approach ensures a consensus on priorities, the efficient use of resources, and the most effective delivery of services to the youth who need them. Multi-disciplinary solutions are key to solving problems in the juvenile justice field.

The Office of Juvenile Justice and Delinquency Prevention's (OJJDP's) anti-gang initiatives exemplify such collaboration. These initiatives bring together a range of community partners to address the multiple risk factors for gang involvement, including poor family management and problematic parent-child relations, low school attachment and achievement, and association with peers who engage in delinquency. Coordinating multiple anti-gang strategies has been shown to offer the highest potential for long-term success in reducing and eliminating gang activity.

Another example of collaboration is the partnership between treatment and justice practitioners in OJJDP-supported juvenile drug court initiatives. Juvenile drug courts not only provide continuous judicial supervision over delinquency and status offense cases that involve substance-abusing juveniles but also, with the assistance of treatment professionals, deliver a range of

OJJDP is working with communities across the country to replicate proven, evidence-based programs and to improve existing programs that address juvenile delinquency. OJJDP supports interventions that respond to the specific developmental, cultural, and gender needs of the youth and families they serve.

services to help these young people. These services include substance abuse and mental health treatment, primary care, and academic support. Because they address the spectrum of problems that often are factors in substance abuse and delinquency, drug courts have proven highly effective in changing individual offender behavior and improving community safety.

These and many of the other activities discussed in this chapter illustrate how OJJDP is helping to coordinate efforts at every level of government and in local communities to offer at-risk and adjudicated youth the most comprehensive and effective services available.

Anti-Gang Initiatives

Gang activity is a complex social phenomenon that varies by age, region, degree of gang involvement, and severity of offending. Risk factors associated with the probability of joining a gang run across family, school, peer, and community lines. Accordingly, no single program or strategy operating independently is likely to have a lasting effect in reducing gang activity. Comprehensive anti-gang initiatives coordinate multiple approaches, recognizing that each strategy plays a role in the overall effort.

OJJDP's fiscal year (FY) 2010 Youth Gang Prevention and Intervention Program awarded nearly $3 million over an 18-month period to 10 sites in Arkansas, California, Connecticut, Florida, Massachusetts, Minnesota, Pennsylvania, and Utah to replicate selected promising or effective anti-gang strategies in targeted communities. A central requirement of the award was that grantees already be a part of an existing comprehensive, community-based anti-gang initiative. The program is designed to reduce violent gang-related incidents in the targeted areas and to improve coordination, planning, and development.

During FY 2010, the Office continued to play a significant role in the delivery of several anti-gang trainings to support the Department of Justice's (DOJ's) Project Safe Neighborhoods. The trainings emphasize the use of data-driven strategies; multidisciplinary partnerships; balanced approaches that include prevention, intervention, and suppression; family and community engagement; and reentry initiatives.

Today, far too many of our children are in need and in pain. Too many kids have given up on themselves and given in to a life of crime. Too many communities are ravaged by gang violence. Too many families have been destroyed. Too many lives have been lost. For me, combating gang violence, and helping children who've been exposed to such violence, has been both a personal and professional concern for decades.

—Attorney General Eric Holder

Evaluation of Gang Reduction Program

OJJDP's Gang Reduction Program (GRP)—a $10 million, multiyear initiative (2003–08) to reduce crime associated with youth street gangs in Los Angeles, CA; Milwaukee, WI; North Miami Beach, FL; and Richmond, VA—used a comprehensive, integrated, and coordinated approach to preventing and reducing gang activity. The program emphasized addressing the needs of youth and affecting change in families, organizations, and communities. The Urban Institute conducted a multiyear evaluation of the GRP initiative in all of the original program sites to assess program implementation and outcomes. Following are selections from the evaluation's findings:

- In contrast to many previous crime prevention and reduction efforts, all sites successfully implemented the GRP model. Three of the four sites also implemented plans to sustain elements of the program as federal funding expired.

- Successful outcomes related to crime reduction were seen in most of the sites, although results varied.

- The strong leadership of a site coordinator, close oversight by OJJDP during the strategic planning and implementation phases, and the availability of technical assistance contributed to implementation progress at the sites.

- GRP is not a one-size-fits-all approach to gang prevention and reduction. The model is flexible enough that sites can adapt it to local conditions yet remain true to the original design.

The GRP evaluation can inform future policy at OJJDP and other federal agencies in successful implementation of a comprehensive anti-gang program. OJJDP published the findings from the evaluation in early FY 2011.

National Gang Center

In October 2009, OJJDP's National Youth Gang Center (NYGC) merged with the National Gang Center (NGC), which is funded by the Office of Justice Programs' (OJP's) Bureau of Justice Assistance. The functions performed by NYGC continue, but its incorporation into an expanded National Gang Center leverages resources more efficiently while enhancing OJJDP's response to the needs of researchers, practitioners, and other concerned citizens. NGC's mission is to expand critical knowledge about gangs and effective strategies to address them. In addition, NGC provides training and technical assistance on community-based responses to gangs and is playing a significant role in DOJ's comprehensive anti-gang efforts.

In FY 2010, NGC released a new bulletin, *History of Street Gangs in the United States,* which reviews the chronology of major historical events associated with the emergence of street gangs in each of four major geographic regions. This publication also places emphasis on older gangs—traditional street gangs—and their involvement in violent criminal activity and other serious crimes.

NGC also conducts the annual National Youth Gang Survey of law enforcement agencies to determine the extent and nature of the nation's gang problem. OJJDP publishes a fact sheet each year summarizing the survey results. Released in FY 2010, *Highlights of the 2008 National Youth Gang Survey* reports that gang activity remains a widespread problem across the United States, with prevalence rates remaining significantly elevated in 2008 compared with recorded lows in the early 2000s.

NGC also maintains a Web site with full-text publications on gang programs and research, a bibliography of gang publications that are not available electronically, lists of gang-related legislation broken down by state and subject, and GANG–INFO, a forum for professionals to exchange information about gangs.

NEW ONLINE TOOL ASSISTS COMMUNITIES IN IMPLEMENTING COMPREHENSIVE GANG MODEL

OJJDP's Comprehensive Gang Model helps communities effectively target areas with high levels of gang activity, define and locate gangs, and focus appropriate resources to address them. The model promotes the interaction of theory, research, and program experience.

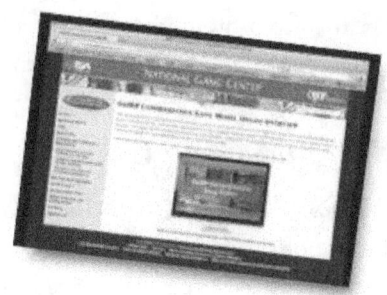

In fiscal year 2010, OJJDP and the National Gang Center created an online tool designed to familiarize state and local organizations with the model. The tool, the Comprehensive Gang Model Overview, provides a 23-minute discussion of OJJDP's model. Key concepts covered include a brief overview of the nation's gang problem, explanation of the theory behind the model and its five core strategies, a discussion about how to effectively assess a gang problem, and tools to assist community leaders in implementing the model in their communities. Transcripts are available for each module. The end of the presentation includes a list of resources and tips to help communities plan for the long-term sustainability of anti-gang programs and strategies.

Community-Based Violence Prevention

In FY 2010, OJJDP created the Community-Based Violence Prevention demonstration program, which uses evidence-based practices to reduce violence in targeted communities. A major focus is serious youth violence and gang violence.

The program aims to change community norms regarding violence, provide alternatives to violence, and increase awareness of the risks and consequences of involvement in violence. An important component of the program is street outreach to intervene in conflicts or potential conflicts and offer nonviolent strategies for resolution. Outreach also involves helping youth find jobs, find a place to live, and receive substance abuse services. The strategies are based on those used in evidence-based models such as the Boston Gun Project, the OJJDP Comprehensive Gang Model, the Richmond Comprehensive Homicide Initiative, and the Chicago CeaseFire model.

In FY 2010, OJJDP awarded more than $8.6 million over a 3-year period to the City and County of Denver Safe City Office (CO); the City of Oakland (CA); the Columbia Heights Shaw Family Support Collaborative (DC); and the Fund for the City of New York/Center for Court Innovation (NY).

BOYS & GIRLS CLUBS OF AMERICA IN UNDERSERVED COMMUNITIES

OJJDP continues its work with Boys & Girls Clubs of America (BGCA) to make a significant and lasting impact on the lives of children living in disadvantaged communities.

In fiscal year (FY) 2010, OJJDP awarded $40 million through its National Mentoring Programs to BGCA to assist local clubs in launching new programs and enhancing existing programs for at-risk youth. To date, this funding has enabled clubs to provide mentoring experiences to more than 83,000 youth, more than 80 percent of whom have completed or are currently participating in an approved evidence-based program designed to reduce substance abuse, crime, and other negative behaviors.

To date, BGCA has provided National Mentoring Programs funding to 105 Boys & Girls Clubs in Indian country and 56 clubs in public housing communities. In addition, the funding supports BGCA Targeted Outreach gang initiatives in 35 communities. Boys & Girls Clubs in 72 communities received funding specifically to develop, implement, and share best-practice strategies for the identification and recruitment of minority male mentors.

Also in FY 2010, OJJDP awarded more than $2 million through the Tribal Youth National Mentoring Program. More than 90 percent of the approximately 2,600 American Indian/Alaska Native (AI/AN) club members who received mentoring have completed or are currently participating in an approved evidence-based program. In addition, technical assistance was offered to all clubs in Indian country, furthering the impact of the grant funds. Approximately 200 Boys & Girls Clubs currently serve 123,000 youth in AI/AN communities in 25 states.

Mentoring Activities

Mentoring is an effective way to prevent at-risk youth from becoming involved in delinquency and also to help delinquent youth change their lives for the better. In FY 2010, OJJDP awarded more than $96.3 million through mentoring appropriations to support the following activities:

New Programs

- The **Multi-State Mentoring Initiative** provides funding for organizations currently operating mentoring programs in five or more states to expand or enhance the capacity of their mentoring initiatives. These initiatives strive to reduce juvenile delinquency and gang participation, improve academic performance, and reduce school dropout rates.

Mentors help young people resist drug use, violence, and delinquency and find what is best in themselves.

—Jeff Slowikowski
Former Acting Administrator,
OJJDP

- The **Mentoring for Safe Schools/Healthy Students (SS/HS) Initiative** seeks to promote the innovative use of mentoring as a component of an existing SS/HS communitywide strategy. The initiative is a joint effort by the U.S. Departments of Education, Health and Human Services, and Justice to support schools and communities in creating safer and healthier learning environments.

New Research and Evaluation Initiatives

- The **Group Mentoring Research and Evaluation Program** evaluates the effectiveness of group mentoring programs supported by local Boys & Girls Clubs. Group mentoring involves one or two mentors working with a group of mentees, rather than one on one. The evaluator will conduct process and outcome evaluations to measure the success of the implementation of these programs and their impact on intervention in and reduction of juvenile delinquency.

- The **Mentoring Research Best Practices Program** seeks to enhance the understanding of mentoring as a prevention strategy for youth who are at risk of involvement or who are already involved in the juvenile justice system. There is a need for research demonstrating the specific components of mentoring programs that have a significant impact in reducing juvenile delinquency and offending. The results of this effort should enhance the implementation of evidence-based practices for juvenile mentoring.

Continuing Programs

- **National Mentoring Programs** support the efforts of national organizations to enhance or expand mentoring services to high-risk populations that are underserved because of location, a shortage of mentors, physical or mental challenges, or other related issues identified by the community.

- The **Second Chance Act Juvenile Mentoring Initiative** provides funding for nonprofit organizations and American Indian/Alaska Native (AI/AN) tribes to develop, implement, and expand mentoring programs and transitional services for juvenile offenders who are reentering their communities after serving a sentence in a correctional facility.

- The **Strategic Enhancement to Mentoring Programs** supports research- and evidence-based enhancements to mentoring programs that involve parents and family in activities and services, deliver structured activities and programs for the mentoring matches, and develop training and support for mentors.

BOYS & GIRLS CLUBS OF GREATER WASHINGTON OBSERVE NATIONAL MENTORING MONTH

In January 2010, OJJDP and the members of the Washington, DC, law enforcement community joined Boys & Girls Clubs of Greater Washington (BGCGW) in observing National Mentoring Month. The event conveyed the theme "Be Mentored, Be Inspired, Be Great: A Celebration in Honor of National Mentoring Month" and provided an overview of mentoring collaboration among OJJDP, BGCGW, and the Washington Metropolitan Police Department.

Speakers at the event included Jeff Slowikowski, then-Acting Administrator, OJJDP; Diane Groomes, Assistant Chief, Metropolitan Police Department; Kevin McCartney, Senior Vice President of Government Relations, Boys & Girls Clubs of America; and Theodore Brannum, Washington, DC, police officer and BGCGW mentor.

Officer Brannum emphasized the significant impact a mentor can have on a young person's life. "Some people ask me why I mentor. The answer is: someone did it for me. I came out of a single-parent home. The people who mentored me left a lasting impression. What we do in the club and the way we live our lives are so important to the kids."

Juvenile Drug Courts

In FY 2010, OJJDP awarded more than $1.2 million over 4 years to jurisdictions in Ohio, Texas, and Washington to implement the Juvenile Drug Court/Reclaiming Futures Program, with training and technical assistance funded and provided by the Robert Wood Johnson Foundation. The FY 2010 funding builds on previous funding of sites in California, Colorado, Missouri, New York, Ohio, and Oklahoma by OJJDP and the U.S. Department of Health and Human Services' Center for Substance Abuse and Treatment.

The Reclaiming Futures Program model offers best practices and specific steps to build the capacity of states, state courts, local courts, units of local government, and tribal governments to help court-involved youth break the destructive cycle of drugs and alcohol and build a better future through education and skills development. The model has been used in 26 communities in 17 states.

Also in FY 2010, OJJDP awarded nearly $3 million for the Juvenile Drug Courts Mentoring and Support Services Initiative. The initiative includes mentoring

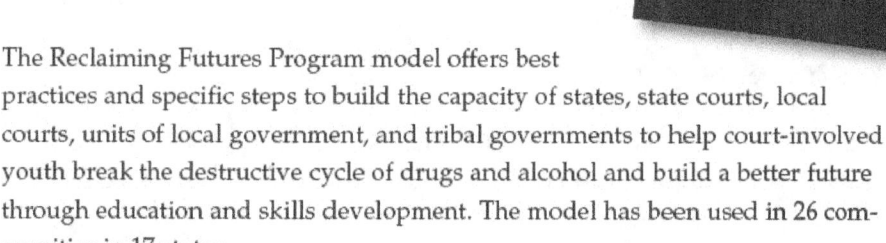

as part of a comprehensive approach to serving substance-abusing youth in juvenile courts. In addition to mentoring, youth are provided with educational, health, employment, and community services; recreational activities; parenting programs; and housing assistance as part of the juvenile drug court approach.

Family Drug Courts

OJJDP's Family Drug Courts program builds the capacity of states, state courts, local courts, units of local government, and Indian tribal governments to implement new and enhance existing drug courts for substance-abusing adults involved with the family dependency court as a result of child abuse and neglect issues. The selected grantees provide services to the children of the parents in the program as well as to the parents. The program's goal is to decrease the incidence of child abuse and neglect, intervene in family risk factors, and reduce the likelihood of negative outcomes for children by addressing parents' substance abuse and providing services to their children.

OJJDP's FY 2010 awards totaled more than $3 million. Eight family drug courts were selected for these awards in California, Georgia, Maryland, Minnesota, Missouri, Montana, North Carolina, and Texas.

Enforcing Underage Drinking Laws Program

OJJDP has administered the Enforcing Underage Drinking Laws (EUDL) program since Congress created the initiative in 1998. The program has four components:

* Block grants awarded to each state and territory and the District of Columbia to improve the enforcement of underage drinking laws.

* Discretionary grants awarded to competitively selected states to support the demonstration of best or promising practices at the local level.

* Training and technical assistance.

* Evaluation.

This section focuses on EUDL's FY 2010 discretionary grants and evaluation activities. (For information on EUDL's block grants and training and technical assistance, see chapter 3.)

For more than a decade, OJJDP has been supporting and enhancing efforts by states and local jurisdictions to prohibit the sale of alcoholic beverages to minors and the purchase and consumption of alcoholic beverages by minors. EUDL discretionary grants support several initiatives, all aimed at helping communities use a comprehensive approach to address underage drinking as well as to document the strategies that are most effective.

Highlights of recent EUDL discretionary programs include partnerships with university/college campuses and adjacent communities to implement research-based and promising practices; a Rural Communities Initiative designed to reduce access, change social norms, and increase enforcement in geographically isolated areas; a Community Trials Initiative to implement and rigorously evaluate the impact of best practices and most promising practices tested in the context of the EUDL program; and a collaboration with the U.S. Air Force to prevent access to and consumption of alcohol by underage military personnel.

OJJDP's partnership with the Air Force currently includes programs in Arizona, California, Hawaii, Montana, Missouri, and Wyoming. The National Institute on Alcohol Abuse and Alcoholism is supporting the program's evaluation, which is being conducted by the Prevention Research Center.

In FY 2010, OJJDP awarded nearly $2.4 million to Maine, Nevada, and Washington for the 3-year EUDL Assessment, Strategic Planning, and Implementation Initiative. The funding will enable these states to conduct an independent assessment of both state and local underage drinking in the first year of the program and to develop a long-range strategic plan based on the independent assessment. Grantees will then implement selected elements of the strategic plan with the goal of decreasing the number of first-time alcohol-related incidents, the incidence of unintentional injuries related to alcohol consumption among underage individuals, and the number of alcohol-related traffic injuries and fatalities involving minors.

Tribal Youth Initiatives

Far too many lives in Indian country have been scarred by violence and crime, as well as by addiction and a lack of learning and job opportunities. Of particular concern to OJJDP is the disproportionate number of violent crimes committed by and against juveniles in Indian country. However, many AI/AN communities lack comprehensive programs to address juvenile delinquency, violence, and other serious problems such as substance abuse and high truancy and dropout rates. In FY 2010, OJJDP entered its 12th consecutive year of congressional appropriations to address these pressing issues.

Coordinated Tribal Assistance Solicitation

In response to concerns that tribes voiced during public listening sessions, in 2010 DOJ developed the Coordinated Tribal Assistance Solicitation (CTAS), which enables federally recognized tribal governments and tribal consortia to submit a single application for all available tribal government-specific grant programs that DOJ offers. Eligible applicants seeking funding for juvenile justice programs in FY 2010 could apply under the following purpose areas: preventing and controlling delinquency and improving the juvenile justice system, enhancing accountability for delinquent behavior, and developing new demonstration projects on violence prevention and rehabilitation.

OJJDP's Tribal Youth Program (TYP) awards grants to federally recognized tribes for activities that prevent juvenile delinquency, reduce violent crime, and improve tribal juvenile justice systems. The program is part of the Indian Country Law Enforcement Initiative, a joint initiative of the U.S. Departments of Justice and the Interior to improve law enforcement and juvenile justice in Indian country. In FY 2010, OJJDP awarded more than $13.4 million to 32 tribal communities through CTAS's two TYP purpose areas.

The Office's Tribal Juvenile Accountability Discretionary Grants Program (T–JADG) provides funds for programs that hold AI/AN youth accountable for their offenses while providing the necessary resources and support for positive outcomes and reduced recidivism. In FY 2010, OJJDP awarded $1.1 million to four tribal communities through CTAS's T–JADG purpose area. (For more information about the T–JADG program, see chapter 3.)

TRIBAL YOUTH FELLOWSHIP

In FY 2010, OJJDP launched a Tribal Youth Fellowship program. The fellowship represents an opportunity for professionals, practitioners, researchers, or trainers with expertise in tribal youth justice to help the federal government improve its partnership with federally recognized tribes on tribal justice matters and in support of tribal children and youth. Among other activities, the fellow has assisted in an effort undertaken through the Coordinating Council on Juvenile Justice and Delinquency Prevention to examine federal tribal youth policy, practice, regulation, and legislation.

"The program provides fellows the opportunity to work closely with federal staff and grantees in a mutually beneficial exchange of information and perspectives," said Jeff Slowikowski, OJJDP's then-Acting Administrator.

For more information on the Coordinating Council's assessment of federal practice in tribal matters and other priority areas, see the section entitled "Interagency Partnerships To Address Key Youth Issues" in chapter 1.

TRIBAL LAW AND ORDER ACT OF 2010

The Tribal Law and Order Act, signed into law by President Barack Obama in July 2010, mandated that the U.S. Departments of Justice (DOJ) and the Interior (DOI) develop, in consultation with tribal leaders and tribal justice professionals, a long-term plan to address incarceration and the alternatives to it in Indian country.

In the ensuing months, DOJ and DOI began working to obtain input from tribal justice officials, including professionals in law enforcement, the courts, and corrections. Consistently, OJJDP's findings pointed to the desire from the field for more alternatives to detention, flexibility in policy and programming that allows tribes to develop strategies that serve their specific public safety needs, and greater coordination among federal, tribal, state, and local government resources to support tribal justice systems. OJJDP produced numerous draft documents with recommendations on juvenile justice issues to inform the Tribal Justice Plan. Those comments were incorporated into a final plan, which was released in FY 2011.

Research suggests that mentoring relationships with caring, responsible, and law-abiding adults may mitigate the risks for delinquency faced by many AI/AN youth. In FY 2010, OJJDP awarded nearly $5.2 million through its Tribal Youth National Mentoring Program to national initiatives that will support the development and expansion of community programs that provide mentoring services to tribal youth populations on reservations of federally recognized tribes across the country. The program focuses on communities that are underserved due to location, a shortage of mentors, emotional or behavioral challenges of the targeted population, or other situations identified by the federally recognized tribes.

Training and Technical Assistance

In FY 2010, OJJDP awarded more than $3.1 million for training and technical assistance to support tribal programming. Approximately $2.4 million was awarded to Education Development Center, Inc., to continue funding the Tribal Youth Training and Technical Assistance Center. The center provides culturally sensitive training and technical assistance to TYP grantees as well as all federally recognized tribes in Indian country. The technical assistance includes access to AI/AN professional staff with expertise in the development of culturally based approaches to prevention and intervention, capacity building, strategic planning, program implementation, program evaluation, and program sustainability.

The Tribal Youth Training and Technical Assistance Center's Web site provides a range of resources, including a calendar of workshops, Webinars, events, and grantee deadlines; funding opportunities; and comprehensive online tools for strategic planning, sustainability, and communications.

TRIBAL YOUTH SUMMIT

In July 2010, DOJ hosted a Tribal Youth Summit at the Institute of American Indian Arts in Santa Fe, NM. More than 110 tribal youth representing 21 tribal communities from across the nation participated. The summit included the first Listening to the Voices of Tribal Youth Circle, in which the youth shared their high-priority concerns with federal officials.

The youth identified alcohol and drug abuse, including prescription drugs; suicide; a lack of productive activities for youth in the community; gang involvement, violence, property theft, and vandalism; and teen pregnancy, among other issues of concern. The goal of the Circle was to create a venue for communication between tribal youth and federal government staff as a tool to shape policy and programs that will affect tribal youth for years to come.

OJJDP also provided its annual regional TYP trainings for grantees in FY 2010. The trainings focused on helping tribes apply their strengths and experiences to develop and maintain programs that are valuable to their communities.

In FY 2010, OJJDP continued to participate in the Tribal Justice Safety and Wellness Training and Technical Assistance initiative launched by the Assistant Attorney General for OJP. This initiative provides training and information to tribal leaders, administrators, program managers, and grant writers on overall resources available from OJP.

Research Activities

Through its Tribal Youth Field-Initiated Research and Evaluation Program, OJJDP awarded $500,000 in FY 2010 to McKinley County, NM, to evaluate the Regional Juvenile Service Center's Alternatives to Detention program, which addresses juvenile delinquency linked with substance abuse. The county's residential social detoxification facility and case management program provide innovative crisis intervention services annually for about 480 youth ages 12 to 17. Previous evaluation studies found that the program reduces juvenile justice involvement and substance abuse for up to 12 months after intake. The evaluation will focus on establishing the efficacy of the program model over a 10-year period, understanding the client characteristics and programmatic features that lead to positive outcomes, and documenting the program for replication in other tribal communities.

Numerous other OJJDP-funded research and evaluation activities continued in FY 2010 to assist the field in better understanding the needs of tribal youth and communities, and in developing effective strategies to address those needs. Following are a few highlights:

- CSR, Inc., is conducting a process evaluation of OJJDP's administration of TYP. OJJDP will use the information from this study to gain a deeper understanding of how federally recognized tribes use the grant funds they are awarded and how OJJDP can better support program implementation and sustainability.

- Prevent Child Abuse America, in partnership with the National Indian Child Welfare Association and other organizations, is conducting research designed to increase knowledge about the severity and extent of tribal youth victimization, tribal adult caregivers' perceptions of youth victimization, and intervention and treatment resources available to tribal youth.

- The National Native Children's Trauma Center is studying the relationship between poverty, a previous history of trauma, and youth violence and substance abuse. The findings from this project are intended to inform the development of a working theory of why violence proliferates in AI/AN communities.

- In collaboration with the Oregon Youth Authority and the Oregon Department of Education, the University of Oregon has developed four model programs to assist youth who are leaving correctional facilities in successfully transitioning back to their communities. An evaluation will measure the impact of the programs on systems change and youth achievement.

CHAPTER 3

CHAPTER 3

OJJDP Is
Strengthening the Juvenile Justice System Through the JJDP Act

Congress established the Office of Juvenile Justice and Delinquency Prevention (OJJDP) and created the Formula Grants program in 1974 to support local and state efforts to prevent delinquency and improve the juvenile justice system. The Formula Grants program provides funds directly to participating states to help them implement the four core requirements of the Juvenile Justice and Delinquency Prevention (JJDP) Act of 1974, as amended:[2]

- Deinstitutionalize status offenders (DSO).

- Separate juveniles from adults in secure facilities (separation).

- Remove juveniles from adult jails and lockups (jail removal).

- Reduce disproportionate minority contact (DMC) within the juvenile justice system.[3]

---

[2] In this chapter, the term "states" also encompasses the five U.S. territories and the District of Columbia. Wyoming does not participate in the Formula Grants program.

[3] In 1988, Congress first required states participating in the Formula Grants program to reduce the disproportionate number of minority youth confined in secure facilities. The issue was elevated to a core requirement in 1992, and then broadened in 2002 to encompass disproportionate representation of minorities at any point in the juvenile justice system.

Long a leader in helping to find solutions to the problem of disproportionate minority contact with the juvenile justice system, OJJDP continues to increase the scope of its resources—including training, technical assistance, publications, and research activities—to help states address this issue.

compliance with the four core requirements as part of its annual Formula Grants State Plan. A state's level of compliance with each of the core protections determines eligibility for its continued participation in the Formula Grants program.

Fulfilling the core requirements is essential to creating a fair, consistent, and effective juvenile justice system that advances the important goals of the JJDP Act.[4]

During fiscal year (FY) 2010, OJJDP worked with the 50 states, the District of Columbia, and the territories to provide financial and technical assistance to support the implementation of the JJDP Act's requirements. The Office also worked with states to help them implement accountability-based reforms; develop collaborative, community-based delinquency prevention programs; and prevent the purchase and consumption of alcohol by minors. These activities are helping states realize the importance of forming partnerships and leveraging a variety of resources to help make a difference for youth by strengthening the juvenile justice system.

---

[4] On March 24, 2009 (during the 111th Congress), Senator Patrick Leahy introduced the Juvenile Justice and Delinquency Prevention Reauthorization Act of 2009 (S. 678). On December 17, 2009, the Senate Judiciary Committee passed the reauthorization bill and sent it to the full Senate for consideration. In addition, the Juvenile Justice and Delinquency Prevention Reauthorization Act of 2010 (H.R. 6029) was introduced by Representative Keith Ellison with cosponsor Representative Robert C. "Bobby" Scott on July 30, 2010. This bill was referred to both the House Committee on Education and Labor and the House Committee on the Judiciary. At the conclusion of the 111th Congress in December 2010, both S. 678 and H.R. 6029 expired without further action. To obtain copies of these bills, go to thomas.loc.gov.

Formula Grants Program

OJJDP awarded approximately $60 million in Formula Grant funds to designated state agencies in FY 2010. During that same period, OJJDP made programmatic site visits to states, completed compliance monitoring audits, provided technical assistance, and sponsored numerous training conferences to assist states in implementing comprehensive juvenile justice plans and programs to prevent delinquency and improve their juvenile justice systems.

In FY 2010, OJJDP's National Training and Technical Assistance Center (NTTAC) provided training and technical assistance to more than 3,155[5] participants in 35 states for the Formula Grants program. The top five topic areas were compliance monitoring, disproportionate minority contact, delinquency prevention, juvenile justice systems improvement, and mental health. Participants included professionals working in child and family services, corrections/detention, law enforcement, juvenile courts, legal services, education, health services, information technology, the private sector, and research.

Also in FY 2010, OJJDP hosted a training day for new juvenile justice specialists, compliance monitors, and disproportionate minority contact coordinators. Held in October in Jersey City, NJ, the training provided information and supporting materials to assist key state agency staff in implementing the federal juvenile justice grant programs administered by OJJDP's State Relations and Assistance Division and ensuring compliance with the four core requirements of the JJDP Act. The training day was led by members of OJJDP's disproportionate minority contact team in collaboration with other expert consultants.

Additional trainings were held in Iowa, Massachusetts, Nebraska, New Hampshire, New Jersey, South Carolina, and Utah in FY 2010. Topics included implementing OJJDP's DMC Reduction Model, strategic planning for State Advisory Groups and their DMC subcommittees, and developing plans to conduct DMC assessment studies. OJJDP also conducted topical Webinars and bimonthly conference calls in FY 2010 with state and local coordinators to provide an opportunity for networking and information sharing.

Performance Measures

Performance measurement is a system of tracking the progress of chosen activities in accomplishing specific goals, objectives, and outcomes. There are two

---

[5] Please note that the number of participants is based on evaluation forms received. The actual number of participants trained may be higher.

types of performance indicators: output and outcome. Output indicators measure the products of a program's implementation or activities. Examples include the number of juveniles served, hours of service provided, staff trained, materials distributed, reports written, and site visits conducted. Outcome indicators measure the benefits or changes for individuals, the juvenile justice system, or the community as a result of the program. Examples include changes in academic performance, prosocial behavior, recidivism rate, and conditions of confinement in detention.

In 2010, states and territories receiving Formula Grant funds reported data for a total of 1,634 awards, including 1,340 subgrants across more than 968 separate organizations. This represents more than $82 million in funded activities. Funds were allocated to activities across many program areas; program areas with the largest funding allocations included:

* Disproportionate minority contact (17 percent).

* Delinquency prevention (16 percent).

* Compliance monitoring (state level) (10 percent).

The program areas selected by the largest number of states included:

* Delinquency prevention (22 percent).

* Disproportionate minority contact (16 percent).

* Alternatives to detention (7 percent).

Formula grant programs served more than 192,000 youth during the reporting period. Of these youth:

* Seventy-two percent completed program requirements.

* Sixty-three percent exhibited a desired change in the targeted behavior.[6]

* Three percent offended or reoffended during the program period.

Of the Formula Grant-funded programs, about 44 percent reported implementing at least one evidence-based program, up from 34 percent for the previous year.

---

[6] Targeted behaviors differed depending on the youth's specific program goals. In the majority of cases, Formula Grant-funded programs targeted a reduction in antisocial behavior, improved school attendance, or increased social competence.

Compliance Progress

In FY 2010, OJJDP continued its work with the states to help them achieve compliance with the core requirements and provide state agencies with training to meet these requirements. To this end, OJJDP supported several technical assistance and training activities related to compliance monitoring in FY 2010. This included specialized onsite training and technical assistance to train new state compliance monitors and to assist states seeking to maintain or achieve compliance with one or more of the core requirements. OJJDP also sponsored specialized compliance training for the U.S. territories and for American Indian/Alaska

MODEL PROGRAMS GUIDE

OJJDP's Model Programs Guide (MPG) is a user-friendly, online portal of scientifically tested, evidence-based programs that address a wide range of issues across the juvenile justice spectrum, from prevention through aftercare. The MPG profiles more than 200 prevention and intervention programs and helps communities identify those that best suit their needs. Users can search the database by program category, target population, risk and protective factors, effectiveness rating, program type, and other characteristics.

In 2007, OJJDP added strategies and programs that show promise in helping jurisdictions reduce disproportionate minority contact in their juvenile justice systems. In 2009, OJJDP completed another expansion to include strategies and programs that help jurisdictions identify and implement evidence-based initiatives leading to the removal of status offenders from secure detention and from correctional facilities.

In 2010, to support the Attorney General's Defending Childhood initiative, the MPG project concentrated on reviewing evidence-based strategies for reducing the impact of children's exposure to violence (CEV). Working with OJJDP's Safe Start Center, CEV subject-matter experts reviewed and rated more than 40 CEV programs. (For more information on the Defending Childhood initiative, see chapter 4.)

Through a partnership with the U.S. Departments of Health and Human Services, Education, and Housing and Urban Development as well as nine other federal agencies, OJJDP makes the programs in the MPG available through the FindYouthInfo.gov Web site. FindYouthInfo.gov was created by the Interagency Working Group on Youth Programs to support programs and services concentrating on youth, with a special emphasis on bullying prevention programs. As part of this partnership, MPG expert reviewers evaluate all program nominations received through the FindYouthInfo.gov Web site.

Native (AI/AN) tribes. As part of ongoing efforts to strengthen compliance monitoring overall, OJJDP also hosted a "training of trainers" session for compliance monitoring in October 2010.

In FY 2010, most states were qualified to receive the maximum amount of Formula Grant funds on the basis of compliance status. (For more compliance information, see appendix B.)

State progress toward achieving the goals of the JJDP Act has been significant. However, the hard work of sustaining that progress remains. OJJDP continues to work to strengthen its program of training and technical assistance to help states address compliance issues.

DMC Activities

Reducing DMC within the juvenile justice system is a requirement for all states that wish to receive grants under the JJDP Act of 1974, as amended. States have made notable progress in addressing DMC. For example, 69 percent of states currently collect and analyze data by race and ethnicity for at least six of the nine juvenile justice system contact points. In addition, more than 89 state and local delinquency prevention and systems improvement activities have been designated as best practices.

FY 2010 was a productive year for the DMC initiative:

- OJJDP completed the annual review of DMC compliance plans for all 50 states, 4 U.S. territories, and the District of Columbia.

- OJJDP continued the Relative Rate Index Modification Project with the Bureau of Justice Statistics and Dr. William Feyerherm of Portland State University to examine how jurisdictions, particularly the U.S. territories and the District of Columbia, can determine the extent of disproportionality when the "minority is the majority."

- OJJDP issued an enhanced technical assistance proposal for the Community and Strategic Planning initiative to facilitate state and local DMC initiatives. Targeted DMC reduction sites will engage in community capacity-building activities that include implementing a community collaborative, conducting a local assessment, and assisting the state DMC coordinator with monitoring delinquency prevention and systems improvement activities.

- OJJDP continues to collaborate with the U.S. Department of Justice's Civil Rights Division to identify local jurisdictions to determine whether high rates of DMC contribute to violations under the Civil Rights of Institutionalized Persons Act.

FACT SHEET ON DISPROPORTIONATE MINORITY CONTACT

In FY 2010, OJJDP released *Disproportionate Minority Contact,* a fact sheet that provides an overview of the Office's efforts to reduce disproportionate minority contact (DMC). The publication includes a description of OJJDP's DMC Reduction Model, which helps states determine whether disproportionality exists and, if it does, guides the establishment of multipronged intervention strategies to ensure equal treatment of all youth. The fact sheet also includes a summary of states' DMC-reduction activities derived from compliance plans submitted in FY 2008.

In response to state DMC coordinators' concerns about disproportional representation of AI/AN youth, OJJDP convened an interagency workgroup with representation from the Bureau of Justice Statistics, the Bureau of Indian Affairs, and the Justice Research and Statistics Association. The workgroup's goals are to determine the extent of DMC (particularly in states with significant AI/AN populations), to further examine how AI/AN youth are processed compared with other minority youth, to ascertain how cultural needs are addressed, and to identify existing promising delinquency prevention and systems improvement strategies.

Juvenile Accountability Block Grants Program

The Juvenile Accountability Block Grants (JABG) program[7] helps states[8] and units of local government improve their juvenile justice systems by implementing accountability-based programs that focus on both juvenile offenders and

---

[7] The House of Representatives passed the Juvenile Accountability Incentive Block Grants (JAIBG) Act in 1997 under Title III of H.R. 3. Congress first funded the program through an appropriations act in fiscal year (FY) 1998. OJJDP, as a component of the Office of Justice Programs within the U.S. Department of Justice, is the administering agency. The Department of Justice Authorization Act of FY 2003 included provisions to change the name of the JAIBG program to the Juvenile Accountability Block Grants (JABG) program, expand the number (from 12 to 16) and scope of the purpose areas, refine the program's reporting and monitoring requirements, and include funding of the program as part of Title I (Part R, Chapter 46, Subchapter XII–F) of the Omnibus Crime Control and Safe Streets Act. Congress added a 17th program area—reentry—in 2006. This report meets the reporting requirements spelled out in the Omnibus Crime Control Act. In addition to being eligible for JABG funds as a state-designated agency, American Indian tribes, as defined by Section 102 of the Federally Recognized Indian Tribe List Act of 1994 (25 U.S.C. 479a), or a consortia of such tribes, are eligible for JABG funding through OJJDP's Tribal Juvenile Accountability Discretionary Grants (T–JADG) program. OJJDP awards T–JADG grants on a competitive basis.

[8] In the context of this report, the term "states" includes the 50 states, the District of Columbia, and the five U.S. territories (American Samoa, Guam, the Northern Mariana Islands, Puerto Rico, and the U.S. Virgin Islands).

ALTERNATIVES TO JUVENILE DETENTION

In FY 2010, OJJDP entered into a partnership with the Annie E. Casey Foundation to jointly fund an expansion of the foundation's Juvenile Detention Alternatives Initiative (JDAI) to additional sites over 2 years. The partnership includes OJJDP funding to support training and technical assistance through three organizations—the W. Haywood Burns Institute, the Center for Children's Law and Policy, and the National Partnership for Juvenile Services—to the new sites implementing the initiative.

Launched in 1992, JDAI assists states and communities across the country in creating and testing new alternatives to detention. At its essence, JDAI demonstrates that jurisdictions can safely reduce their reliance on secure detention. JDAI communities also test the hypothesis that detention reforms will equip juvenile justice systems with values, skills, and policies that will improve results in other components of the system. The objectives of JDAI sites are to eliminate the inappropriate or unnecessary use of secure detention, minimize rearrest and failure-to-appear rates pending adjudication, ensure appropriate conditions of confinement in secure facilities, redirect public finances to sustain successful reforms, and reduce racial and ethnic disparities. Another highlight of 2010 was the Annie E. Casey Foundation's JDAI summit for tribal detention centers, held in October.

Today, JDAI reform efforts are underway in more than 125 jurisdictions in 30 states and the District of Columbia. OJJDP is also supporting an evaluation of the JDAI approach and its impact in furthering the deinstitutionalization of status offenders, a core requirement under the JJDP Act.

the juvenile justice system. Accountability means holding a juvenile who has violated the law responsible for the behavior by imposing consequences commensurate with the seriousness of the offense and the youth's previous criminal history. These sanctions can include restitution, community service, victim-offender mediation, probation, electronic monitoring, incarceration, and reentry services. JABG monies also fund training and technical assistance to enhance the ability of the state and local juvenile justice systems to maintain and enhance intervention and treatment programs, track offenders, and process cases in a timely manner.

OJJDP distributed more than $46 million in funds in FY 2010 under the JABG program to the 50 states, the District of Columbia, and the U.S. territories.

Recipients must use their JABG funds to support activities in 1 of 17 purpose areas (see the sidebar, "Juvenile Accountability Block Grants Program Purpose Areas"). The purpose areas are centered on four types of activities—hiring staff, building infrastructure, implementing programs, and training staff.

OJJDP provides training and technical assistance through three providers:

* NTTAC provides training and technical assistance to the states and territories. The requests for JAGB training that NTTAC received in FY 2010 were concentrated in the following areas: graduated sanctions; training for law enforcement, court, and probation officers; reentry; restorative justice; sustainability; and juvenile drug courts.

* CSR, Inc., manages the data collection and technical assistance tool, known as DCTAT, that states use when submitting JABG performance measurement data. CSR staff also provide training and support on the use of the JABG performance measures.

* The JABG Technical Support Center, established by OJJDP with assistance from the Bureau of Justice Statistics and a grant to the Justice Research and Statistics Association, provides states the data they need to calculate JABG allocations for local jurisdictions.

During the 2010 JABG reporting period (October 1, 2009, to September 30, 2010), OJJDP provided 15 JABG training and technical assistance events to 240[9] individuals from 10 states and the District of Columbia. This support was in the form of workshops, conference presentations, funding, resource identification, and curriculum development. Training participants included probation officers, substance abuse treatment providers, family advocates, judges, clerks and court staff, juvenile justice residential and detentions staff, members of community organizations, and state advisory group members.

JABG Results

States and units of local government report their performance data on an annual reporting cycle. A reporting cycle consists of a 12-month reporting period, followed by a 3-month period in which data must be submitted. For example, grantees and subgrantees collected JABG data during the reporting period April 1, 2009, to March 31, 2010, and submitted it through June 30, 2010. Hereafter, the reporting period will be referred to as the 2010 reporting period.

---

[9] Please note that the number of participants is based on evaluation forms received. The actual number of participants trained may be higher.

JUVENILE ACCOUNTABILITY BLOCK GRANTS PROGRAM PURPOSE AREAS

Purpose Area	Description of Purpose Area
1. Graduated sanctions	Developing, implementing, and administering graduated sanctions for juvenile offenders.
2. Corrections/detention facilities	Building, expanding, renovating, or operating temporary or permanent juvenile corrections, juvenile detention, or community corrections facilities.
3. Court staffing and pretrial services	Hiring juvenile court judges, probation officers, court-appointed defenders, and special advocates and funding pretrial services for juvenile offenders to promote the effective and expeditious administration of the juvenile justice system.
4. Prosecutors (staffing)	Hiring additional prosecutors so that more cases involving violent juvenile offenders can be prosecuted and case backlogs can be reduced.
5. Prosecutors (funding)	Providing funding to enable prosecutors to address drug, gang, and youth violence problems more effectively. Providing funding for technology, equipment, and training to help prosecutors identify and expedite the prosecution of violent juvenile offenders.
6. Training for law enforcement and court personnel	Establishing and maintaining training programs for law enforcement and other court personnel with respect to preventing and controlling juvenile crime.
7. Juvenile gun courts	Establishing juvenile gun courts for the prosecution and adjudication of juvenile firearms offenders.
8. Juvenile drug courts	Establishing drug court programs for juvenile offenders that provide continuing judicial supervision over juvenile offenders with substance abuse problems and integrate the administration of other sanctions and services for such offenders.
9. Juvenile records systems	Establishing and maintaining a system of juvenile records designed to promote public safety.
10. Information sharing	Establishing and maintaining interagency information-sharing programs that enable the juvenile and criminal justice systems, schools, and social services agencies to make more informed decisions about the early identification, control, supervision, and treatment of juveniles who repeatedly commit serious delinquent or criminal acts.
11. Accountability	Establishing and maintaining accountability-based programs designed to reduce recidivism among juveniles who are referred by law enforcement personnel or agencies.
12. Risk and needs assessment	Establishing and maintaining programs to conduct risk and needs assessments that facilitate effective early intervention and help provide comprehensive services (including mental health and substance abuse screening and treatment) to juvenile offenders.
13. School safety	Establishing and maintaining accountability-based programs that are designed to enhance school safety. These programs may include research-based bullying, cyberbullying, and gang prevention programs.
14. Restorative justice	Establishing and maintaining restorative justice programs.
15. Juvenile courts and probation	Establishing and maintaining programs to enable juvenile courts and juvenile probation officers to be more effective and efficient in holding juvenile offenders accountable and reducing recidivism.
16. Corrections/detention personnel	Hiring detention and corrections personnel, and establishing and maintaining training programs for such personnel to improve facility practices and programming.
17. Reentry	Establishing, improving, and coordinating prerelease and postrelease systems and programs to facilitate the successful reentry of juvenile offenders from state and local custody in the community.

Performance Measures

To assess the effectiveness of the JABG program, OJJDP developed a set of performance measures that help the Office, Congress, and the juvenile justice field see the progress and challenges facing the program. During FY 2010, OJJDP continued to work with the states to collect quantitative performance measures data.

This section presents the performance data for the 2010 reporting period, representing information that states collected from their subgrantees.[10]

All grantees submitted at least some performance data. States reported performance data for 1,373 subgrants, representing approximately $74 million in funded activities.

During the 2010 reporting period, the JABG grantees and subgrantees reported performance measures data regarding activities that were funded by active awards received in FYs 2004 through 2009. Although funds were allocated to activities across all 17 JABG purpose areas, the activities with the largest funding allocations included:

* Accountability-based programs (26 percent).

* Court/probation programming (14 percent).

* Risk/needs assessments (9 percent).

JABG programs served more than 300,000 youth during the 2010 reporting period. The following is summary information about the performance of JABG grantees and subgrantees:

* Seventy-seven percent of program youth successfully completed program requirements (148,050 of 191,369 youth who exited the program).

* Sixty percent of program youth exhibited a desired change in targeted behavior (113,187 of 189,390 youth served).[11]

* Twenty-six percent of programs reported using an evidence-based program or practice (364 of 1,374 programs), up from 21 percent in 2009.

---

[10] The final responsibility for the accuracy and validity of these data rests with the state/territorial JABG grantees who submitted them to OJJDP.

[11] Targeted behaviors differed depending on the youth's specific program goals. In the majority of cases, JABG programs targeted a reduction in antisocial behavior, improved school attendance, or increased social competence.

- Seven percent of program youth reoffended during the program period (50 of 1,393 youth served), down from 20 percent in 2009.

SUCCESS STORY: JABG PROGRAM

Project Connect (South Carolina)

Carolina Family Services, Inc.'s Project Connect offers a community-based and culturally competent alternative to secure detention. The project provides approximately 75 juveniles who have committed mild to moderate offenses and their families with family advocates immediately after arrest to address factors influencing the juvenile's delinquent behavior.

During the 12-week program, family advocates work to strengthen parenting skills and help the family access community resources, including mental health or substance abuse services, individual and family therapy, and recreational, social, educational, and vocational programs. An individualized treatment plan identifies each family's specific strengths and weaknesses in different areas, targets specific goals, and outlines the steps necessary to achieve those goals.

Ninety-five percent of the youth/families enrolling during the period April 1, 2009, through October 31, 2010, who completed the program were considered successful on all outcome measures. They demonstrated an increase in social skills development, school attendance, grade point average, positive family relationships, and family functioning.

Tribal Juvenile Accountability Discretionary Grants Program

The Tribal Juvenile Accountability Discretionary Grants program (T–JADG) funds programs that hold AI/AN youth accountable for their offenses and provides the necessary resources and support for positive outcomes and reduced recidivism. T–JADG funds are a separate allocation within the JABG appropriation. OJJDP awards T–JADG cooperative agreements to federally recognized tribes through a competitive process.

Through the Department of Justice's (DOJ's) Coordinated Tribal Assistance Solicitation, in FY 2010 OJJDP awarded T–JADG grants—a total of more than $1 million—to four tribes: Lac du Flambeau Band of Lake Superior Chippewa Indians (Wisconsin), Yurok Tribe (California), Gila River Indian Community (Arizona), and Pueblo of Jemez (New Mexico).

Performance Measures

In FY 2010, OJJDP had 13 active T–JADG awards, representing more than $3.9 million in funding. Of the 13 T–JADG grantees, 12 provided performance data for the 2010 reporting period. Data for 2010 include the following:

- Ninety-five percent of program youth exhibited a desired change in targeted behavior (1,593 of 1,671), up from 59 percent in 2009.[12]

FEDERAL ADVISORY COMMITTEE ON JUVENILE JUSTICE

OJJDP obtains advice and guidance from the states, the territories, and the District of Columbia through the Federal Advisory Committee on Juvenile Justice (FACJJ). FACJJ is an advisory body established by the Juvenile Justice and Delinquency Prevention Act of 1974, as amended (Section 223), and is supported by OJJDP. Its role is to advise the President and

Congress on matters related to juvenile justice and delinquency prevention, to advise the OJJDP Administrator on the work of OJJDP, and to evaluate the progress and accomplishments of juvenile justice activities and projects.

As of FY 2010, FACJJ included appointed representatives from the State Advisory Groups of each of the 50 states, the District of Columbia, and the territories. FACJJ's mandated responsibilities include preparing two annual recommendation reports—one to the President and Congress, and one to the Office.

FACJJ's first meeting in FY 2010 was held October 29–31, 2009, in Austin, TX. The meeting included presentations on law enforcement approaches to disproportionate minority contact with the juvenile justice system, roundtable discussions with OJJDP leadership on key issues, and a discussion of options for reconfiguring FACJJ in the future.

At FACJJ's spring meeting, held May 10–12, 2010, in Washington, DC, discussions focused on the status of reauthorization of the Juvenile Justice and Delinquency Prevention Act, the Committee's 2010 annual reports, and the Coordinating Council on Juvenile Justice and Delinquency Prevention's current analysis of the impact that federal policies, regulations, and practices related to youth programs have on states and communities.

---

[12] Targeted behaviors differed depending on the youth's specific program goals. In the majority of cases, T–JADG programs targeted a reduction in antisocial behavior, improved school attendance, or increased social competence.

- Seventy-nine percent of program youth successfully completed program requirements (104 of 131), up from 74 percent in 2009.

- Fifty-four percent of programs reported using an evidence-based program or practice (7 of 13 programs).

Community Prevention Grants Program

Preventing young people from engaging in delinquent behavior, thus diverting many of them from a lifetime of criminal activity, is a central goal of the juvenile justice system in this country. Since 1994, OJJDP has administered the Community Prevention Grants (CPG) program, which provides funds to help communities develop and implement delinquency prevention programs.[13] The program focuses on helping youth avoid involvement in delinquency through reducing the risk factors and enhancing the protective factors in their schools, communities, and families.

Extensive research has shown that risk factors increase the likelihood that a youth will engage in delinquent behavior, and protective factors help prevent or reduce that likelihood. For example, studies have shown that a lack of engagement in school and persistent family conflicts are highly correlated with adolescent delinquency and violence, among other serious problems. In developing a program to prevent juvenile delinquency, communities often adopt a collaborative approach that includes working with schools and families to help these at-risk youth.

The CPG program encourages local leaders to initiate multidisciplinary needs assessments of the risks and resources in their communities and to develop locally relevant prevention plans that simultaneously draw on community resources, address local gaps in services or risks, and employ evidence-based or theory-driven strategies. Communities may allocate their Title V funds under 1 or more of 19 program areas (see the sidebar, "Community Prevention Grants Program Areas").

In FY 2010, OJJDP awarded $569,156 in grants through the CPG program, with $20,336 going to most states.[14] Although this was a considerably smaller grant award than in previous years, OJJDP reasoned that these allocations, combined with the program requirement of a 50-percent match, would enable states to

---

[13] Congress established the Title V Community Prevention Grants program in its 1992 amendments to the JJDP Act. OJJDP began administering the program in 1994.

[14] In the context of the Community Prevention Grants program, the term "states" includes the 50 states, the District of Columbia, and the 5 U.S. territories (American Samoa, Guam, the Northern Mariana Islands, Puerto Rico, and the U.S. Virgin Islands).

COMMUNITY PREVENTION GRANTS PROGRAM AREAS

Purpose Area	Description of Purpose Area
Child abuse and neglect	Programs that provide treatment to juvenile victims of child abuse or neglect and to their families to reduce the likelihood that such at-risk youth will commit violations of law.
Children of incarcerated parents	Services to prevent delinquency or treat first-time and nonserious delinquent juveniles who are the children of incarcerated parents.
Delinquency prevention	Programs to prevent youth at risk of becoming delinquent from entering the juvenile justice system or to intervene with first-time and nonserious offenders to keep them out of the juvenile justice system. This program area excludes programs targeted at youth already adjudicated delinquent, on probation, or in corrections, and programs undertaken as part of program areas 12 and 32 of the Formula Grants program that are designed specifically to prevent gang-related or substance abuse activities.
Disproportionate minority contact	Delinquency prevention programs primarily to address the disproportionate number of juvenile members of minority groups who come into contact with the juvenile justice system, pursuant to Section 223(a)(22) of the JJDP Act of 1974, as amended.
Diversion	Programs to divert juveniles from entering the juvenile justice system.
Gangs	Programs to address issues related to preventing juvenile gang activity.
Gender-specific services	Services to address the needs of female and male offenders in the juvenile justice system.
Gun programs	Programs to reduce the unlawful acquisition and illegal use of guns by juveniles (excluding programs to purchase guns from juveniles).
Hate crimes	Programs to prevent hate crimes committed by juveniles.
Job training	Projects to enhance the employability of at-risk juveniles and/or first-time and nonserious juvenile offenders or prepare them for future employment (e.g., job readiness training, apprenticeships, and job referrals).
Juvenile system improvement	Programs, research, and other initiatives to examine issues related to the juvenile justice system or to improve existing juvenile justice information-sharing systems.
Mental health services	Psychological and psychiatric evaluations and treatment, counseling services, and/or family support services for at-risk juveniles and/or first-time and nonserious juvenile offenders.
Mentoring	Programs to develop and sustain an ongoing one-to-one supportive relationship between a responsible adult age 18 or older (mentor) and an at-risk juvenile and/or first-time and nonserious juvenile offender (mentee).
American Indian programs	Programs to address delinquency prevention issues for American Indians and Alaska Natives.
Restitution/community service	Programs to hold first-time and nonserious juvenile offenders accountable for their offenses by requiring community service or repayment to the victim.
Rural area juvenile programs	Prevention services in an area located outside a metropolitan statistical area as designated by the U.S. Census Bureau.
School programs	Educational programs and/or related services to prevent truancy, suspension, and expulsion. School safety programs may include support for school resource officers and law-related education.
Substance abuse	Programs to prevent and treat the use and abuse of illegal and other prescription and nonprescription drugs and the use and abuse of alcohol among at-risk juveniles and/or nonserious juvenile offenders.
Youth (or teen) courts	Juvenile justice programs in which peers play an active role in the disposition of first-time and nonserious juvenile offenders. Most communities use youth courts as a sentencing option for first-time offenders charged with misdemeanor or nonserious, nonviolent offenses who acknowledge their guilt. The youth court serves as an alternative to the traditional juvenile court.

fund at least one evidence-based program, thereby retaining the intent of the program to support research-based delinquency prevention efforts.

Training and Technical Assistance

OJJDP offers a three-part training series to help grantees write successful 3-year delinquency prevention plans. The training includes:

* Community team orientation, which brings together key local leaders and provides an overview of the CPG model.

* Community data collection and analysis training, which helps participants review, analyze, prioritize, and present the data they have collected.

* Community planning and program development training, which shows participants how to use data to develop delinquency prevention plans and how to select appropriate strategies using the Model Programs Guide (for more information, see the sidebar, "Model Programs Guide").

Because membership in a community coalition is a prerequisite for funding, training participants included community leaders, program developers, researchers, and others who are involved in mobilizing the community or in governing or serving children.

The Office also provides specialized training in performance measurement and evaluation, evidence-based practices, and sustainability. The training is available to CPG subgrantees, juvenile justice specialists, and state CPG coordinators.

Performance Measures

In FY 2010, 56 grantees submitted at least some performance information to OJJDP. Of those, 52 submitted complete performance data for subgrant awards that were active in FY 2010, using the Title V performance measures. States and territories reported data for a total of 154 active subgrants from 106 subgrantees, representing more than $4 million in funded activities.

Following are the program areas to which the greatest number of subgrants were allocated:

* Delinquency prevention (88 subgrants).

* School programs (28 subgrants).

* Disproportionate minority contact (27 subgrants).

During FY 2010, OJJDP worked with the states to collect quantitative performance measurement data. An analysis of these data shows that in FY 2010, Community Prevention Grants programs served 24,191 youth; 52 percent of youth completed program requirements. Of the 258 local programs that provided performance data during this reporting cycle, 46 percent were evidence based, up from 15 percent in 2009.

These local programs addressed a wide range of youth behaviors. Overall, 58 percent of youth participants in funded programs exhibited positive changes in behavior targeted by the program.[15] More specifically, program participants showed the following improvements in their behavior:

- Thirty-seven percent improved their school attendance.

- Eighty-six percent reduced their antisocial behavior, up from 56 percent in 2009.

- Sixty-eight percent improved relationships with their families.

- Seventy-five percent reduced their substance use, up from 62 percent in 2009.

The ultimate outcome measure for delinquency prevention programs is a low offending rate among program participants. In FY 2010, the offending and reoffending rate of CPG program participants was 1.2 percent and 4.4 percent, respectively, down from 8 percent for both categories in 2009.

● ● ● SUCCESS STORY: COMMUNITY PREVENTION GRANTS PROGRAM

Delinquency Prevention Project (Michigan)

Alpena County's Delinquency Prevention Project was created after the release of data showing a 200-percent spike in first-time alcohol use in county youth ages 11 to 12 and a 35-percent higher rate of substance abuse treatment among young people than in the surrounding 20 counties in southern Michigan. Based on these data, county officials determined that the best course of action was for a Prevention Policy Board (composed of 18 community stakeholders, including the courts, law enforcement, schools, clergy, community agencies, health departments, and individuals) to develop a comprehensive plan to address substance abuse issues.

The goals of the project are to prevent and reduce substance abuse among county youth and to sustain the Prevention Policy Board as the primary entity advancing substance abuse prevention efforts in the county. The project coordinated the implementation of the Botvin Lifeskills curriculum in each of the

---

[15] Targeted behaviors differed depending on the youth's specific program goals. In the majority of cases, CPG programs targeted a reduction in antisocial behavior, improved school attendance, or increased social competence.

county's schools. Through coordination and cooperation among the stakeholders, the project diverted substance abuse prevention funding from a licensed provider, who had offered the services for more than 20 years, to a school-based agency. The project also used Title V funding to conduct the Michigan Profile for Healthy Youth online risk assessment in each school in the county and to provide training in the Botvin Lifeskills curriculum for 18 community-based agency personnel.

About 1,200 students (all fifth through eighth graders in the county) were taught the curriculum. Annual evaluations of the first 3 years in which the curriculum was taught indicated improvements in knowledge about drugs, knowledge about life skills, attitudes toward drugs, drug refusal skills, assertiveness skills, strategies for reducing anxiety, and drug use behavior.

The Prevention Policy Board has exceeded everyone's expectations. Stakeholders are happy with the changes that the process of creating and sustaining the Prevention Policy Board have brought to the community, and they are also satisfied with the collaborative process and cooperation that local government processes and institutions have seen. Stakeholder participation remains high; key community members regularly attend meetings to monitor data, analyze resources and gaps in services, and respond to funding and technical assistance opportunities.

Enforcing Underage Drinking Laws Program

During the past 12 years, OJJDP's Enforcing Underage Drinking Laws (EUDL) program has successfully built partnerships with law enforcement, community organizations, and government officials to implement evidence-based strategies to reduce youth access to alcohol.

The EUDL program includes both block grants and discretionary grants. This chapter focuses on EUDL's block grants and training and technical assistance activities. (For information about EUDL's discretionary grant activities, see chapter 2.)

Under the EUDL block grants program, each state, the District of Columbia, and the territories received more than $356,000 in FY 2010, totaling $20 million. These funds are allocated to enforce state laws prohibiting the sale of alcoholic beverages to minors and to prevent the purchase or consumption of alcoholic beverages by minors.

Activities funded under the EUDL program may include:

* Forming statewide task forces of state and local law enforcement and prosecutorial agencies to target establishments suspected of a pattern of violations of state laws governing the sale and consumption of alcohol by minors.

- Creating public advertising programs to educate establishments about statutory prohibitions and sanctions.

- Developing innovative programs to prevent and combat underage drinking.

EUDL funds support a wide range of activities. Many states focus on enforcement, emphasizing compliance checks of retail alcohol outlets. Other enforcement activities include crackdowns on false identification, programs to deter older youth or adults from providing alcohol to minors, party patrols to prevent drinking at large gatherings, "cops in shops" to keep minors from purchasing alcohol, youth-focused campaigns to enforce impaired driving laws, and investigations to determine the source of alcohol and hold the responsible party accountable for their role in an alcohol-related incident. The funds also support public education programs and innovative methods for reaching youth.

The training and technical assistance component of the EUDL program has been instrumental in helping communities and states enforce underage drinking laws around the country. OJJDP's Underage Drinking Enforcement and Training Center (UDETC), managed by the Pacific Institute for Research and Evaluation, provides training workshops, curriculums, regional meetings, national conferences, onsite strategic technical assistance, and other resources. In FY 2010, UDETC conducted a total of 84 trainings, reaching more than 4,600 individuals in 50 states, the District of Columbia, and the 5 U.S. territories.

The EUDL program held its 12th Annual National Leadership Conference in Anaheim, CA, in August 2010. The conference addressed a variety of topics related to the prevention of underage drinking and the effective enforcement of underage drinking laws. A special youth track also was included. Plenary sessions, workshops, and experiential learning exercises provided participants with information, skills, and tools for use in enhancing local efforts. The conference highlighted communities, programs, and other initiatives that have successfully implemented evidence-based strategies to reduce youth's access to alcohol.

Performance Measures

During the activity period January 1 to December 31, 2010, states and territories reported data for a total of 1,034 EUDL subgrants across 616 separate organizations. In this period, states and territories reported data for approximately $54 million in subgrant and statewide awards. Nationally, funds were allocated to four program categories: coalitions; media; enforcement; and education, training, and other activities. Twenty-one percent of subgrants focused on coalitions, 23 percent on media, 49 percent on enforcement, and 7 percent on education, training, and other activities.

Performance data for this reporting period indicate some positive trends:

- Seventy-five percent of funded projects are using an evidence-based model.

- Thirty-eight percent of task forces and coalitions addressing underage drinking in states were created as a result of EUDL funding.

- Eighty-seven percent of off-premise alcohol establishments checked during this reporting period were in compliance (27,543 of 31,829 establishments), up from 81 percent in 2009.

- Eighty-eight percent of on-premise alcohol establishments checked were in compliance (19,165 of 21,776), up from 84 percent in 2009.

- A total of 19,638 adult citations were issued during enforcement operations conducted during this reporting period.

- A total of 45,818 youth were involved in task force and coalition leadership activities.

SUCCESS STORY: EUDL PROGRAM

Liquor Control Board Adopts Alcohol Advertising Restrictions (Washington)

Many advertisements portray alcohol as a way of having fun and as a sign of prosperity and social popularity. These messages avoid alerting youth to the risks associated with alcohol use, including crime, suicide, and traffic injuries and fatalities. Communities across the country are struggling to find ways to shield youth from these misleading advertisements.

The state of Washington's Enforcing Underage Drinking Laws (EUDL) program (through RUaD, its statewide collation to reduce underage drinking) responded to this problem with an "action kit" that provides tools and resources to help communities reduce alcohol marketing to youth. Funding from the EUDL program supported the pilot testing of the action kit in five communities. The kit was then widely distributed throughout the state. In addition, RUaD's cochair, also a member of Washington State's Liquor Control Board (LCB), saw an opportunity for LCB to enhance public safety by revising its administrative code related to alcohol advertising. Many meetings, policy drafts, and public hearings followed. At the final public hearing at LCB's headquarters in February 2010, the room was filled with students, professionals, and citizens who traveled from locations across the state to testify in favor of the proposed revisions. In March, LCB adopted revisions that restrict the size, amount, and location of alcohol advertising at liquor-licensed locations.

Washington's success in limiting outdoor advertising was the result of collaboration between individuals and organizations across the state, confirming the importance of partnerships in the development of successful strategies for reducing underage drinking.

CHAPTER 4

CHAPTER 4

OJJDP Is
Defending Children Against Victimization

Our nation's children are victimized at an alarming rate. According to the Office of Juvenile Justice and Delinquency Prevention (OJJDP)-funded National Survey of Children's Exposure to Violence (NatSCEV), nearly one-half of youth were assaulted at least once in the past year, and more than 1 in 10 were injured in an assault. Many children are subjected not only to physical violence, but also to mental and sexual abuse. Others are abducted, often by members of their own family. Still others are the victims of theft, vandalism, or bullying.

Even children who are not direct victims can experience long-term adverse effects if they regularly witness violence in their homes, schools, and communities. Research has shown that children who are directly or indirectly exposed to violence are significantly more likely to display a variety of problems during adolescence, including serious and violent delinquency, drug use, mental health problems, and low academic achievement.

The challenge of protecting children has been made significantly more complex by ready access to the Internet. Parents, child protection agencies, and law enforcement are struggling to protect children from the threat of online victimization, which can include pornography, cyberbullying, abduction, sexual abuse, and child prostitution. OJJDP took the lead early on in addressing this serious problem. More than a decade ago, the Office established the Internet Crimes Against Children (ICAC) program, which helps state and local law enforcement agencies prevent,

The challenge of defending children has been made infinitely more complex by ready access to the Internet. Parents, child protection agencies, and law enforcement are struggling to protect children from the threat of online victimization. OJJDP's Internet Crimes Against Children program and the U.S. Department of Justice's Project Safe Childhood have been successful in targeting predators who use cyberspace to entice children.

against children. The task forces use aggressive investigations, prosecutions, computer forensics, and community outreach to address cybercrime.

In addition to ICAC, the Office supports a wide range of programs that promote evidence-based strategies to protect children against abuse, neglect, abduction, commercial sexual exploitation, and exposure to community and domestic violence. OJJDP activities highlighted in this chapter provide a broad picture of how OJJDP is working vigorously with communities, law enforcement, and social service agencies to ensure the safety and well-being of our nation's children.

Children's Exposure to Violence

NatSCEV revealed that more than 60 percent of the nation's youth had been exposed to violence, crime, or abuse within the past year, either directly or indirectly. Almost 40 percent were direct victims of two or more violent acts. One in four was a victim of robbery, vandalism, or theft. One in sixteen was victimized sexually. One in four witnessed a violent act. And almost 1 in 10 saw a family member assault another family member.

NatSCEV is conducted by the University of New Hampshire's Crimes against Children Research Center and is sponsored by OJJDP and the Centers for Disease Control and Prevention. It is the first comprehensive attempt to measure children's exposure to violence in the home, school, and community across age groups from birth through age 17 and the cumulative exposure to violence over a child's lifetime.

In October 2009, OJJDP released the study's findings in the bulletin, *Children's Exposure to Violence: A Comprehensive National Survey.* "Those numbers are astonishing, and they are unacceptable," Attorney General Eric Holder said at the time of the publication's release. "We simply cannot stand for an epidemic of violence that robs our youth of their childhood and perpetuates a cycle in which today's victims become tomorrow's criminals."

To address this serious issue, in September 2010 Attorney General Holder announced a new initiative, Defending Childhood, which aims to prevent exposure to violence, mitigate the negative effects experienced by children exposed to violence, and

develop knowledge about and spread awareness of this issue. The initiative involves public and private partners and leverages federal resources and funding within the Department of Justice (DOJ) and throughout the government. Fiscal year (FY) 2010 funding for the initiative totaled $5.5 million.

A key component of the Defending Childhood initiative is a two-phase, multi-year demonstration program. Phase I includes planning grants for eight demonstration sites: the City of Boston, MA; the City of Portland, ME; the Chippewa Cree Tribe, MT; the City of Grand Forks, ND; the Cuyahoga County Board of Commissioners, OH; the Multnomah County Department of Human Services, OR; the Rosebud Sioux Tribe, SD; and Shelby County, TN. In FY 2010, OJJDP awarded grants for this project totaling $1.27 million.

The grantees will work in collaboration with other local organizations to develop comprehensive community-based strategies to prevent and reduce the impact of children's exposure to violence in their homes, schools, and communities. In addition to the demonstration program grants, DOJ committed additional funding for research, evaluation, public awareness, and partnerships related to the initiative.

Training and technical assistance will be provided by the Safe Start Center, DOJ's national resource center for information and training related to reducing children's exposure to violence. OJJDP funding for the Center's training and technical assistance totaled $2.4 million in FY 2010, including support for the Defending Childhood initiative.

FELLOWSHIP IN CHILDREN'S EXPOSURE TO VIOLENCE

In fiscal year 2010, OJJDP awarded a 1-year fellowship in children's exposure to violence (CEV). The CEV fellow works onsite at OJJDP in Washington, DC. The fellow supports OJJDP's efforts in the area of children's exposure to violence by collaborating with practitioners, researchers, and trainers with expertise in children's exposure to violence to help implement cross-agency strategies, policies, and evidence-based practices.

Among other activities, the fellow supports OJJDP's Safe Start Center and the U.S. Department of Justice's new Defending Childhood initiative by helping design, develop, and assess initiatives and training programs; conduct research and evaluations; develop policy; and engage in outreach and awareness activities. The fellow also assists in the development of reports and publications.

In FY 2010, OJJDP continued its partnership with the RAND Corporation and 15 communities to collect and disseminate process and outcome data on interventions for children exposed to violence. In the spring of 2010, the RAND Corporation released the findings of the process evaluation, which synthesized information across all 15 sites to describe the program and community settings, interventions, and implementation. The evaluation documented the sites' success in launching programs and delivering high-quality and needed services to children exposed to violence. At the same time, most programs faced difficulties obtaining referrals and engaging families in treatment because of the very complex needs of these vulnerable families. These and the evaluation's other findings will serve as a useful tool in future efforts to develop community-based programs for children exposed to violence.

In the summer of 2010, OJJDP added 10 new sites and provided a total of $2.5 million for intervention services for families. In addition, OJJDP awarded approximately $765,000 to the RAND Corporation to continue research on promising interventions and a national evaluation of the strategies implemented at these new sites.

OJJDP also awarded new grant funds of approximately $1.1 million to the Crimes against Children Research Center to expand and continue NatSCEV. The center's researchers will conduct a longitudinal analysis of participants in the original NatSCEV survey, develop trend data on a new group of survey participants, and create a toolkit to help communities accurately measure the incidence, nature, and extent of children's exposure to violence.

Project Safe Childhood

DOJ established the Project Safe Childhood (PSC) initiative in May 2006 to combat the proliferation of technology-facilitated sexual exploitation crimes against children. PSC combines law enforcement efforts, community action, and public awareness. Local PSC coalitions, which are led by U.S. Attorneys' Offices, have as a key component the OJJDP-supported ICAC task forces, which are tasked with investigating, apprehending, and prosecuting individuals who exploit children via the Internet, as well as identifying and rescuing victims. For more information on the ICAC program, see the section, "Internet Crimes Against Children Program" below.

ATTORNEY GENERAL ANNOUNCES NATIONAL STRATEGY FOR CHILD EXPLOITATION PREVENTION AND INTERDICTION

In August 2010, Attorney General Eric Holder announced the U.S. Department of Justice's (DOJ's) National Strategy for Child Exploitation Prevention and Interdiction. The strategy provides the first-ever comprehensive threat assessment of the dangers facing children from child pornography, online enticement, child sex tourism, commercial sexual exploitation, and sexual exploitation in Indian country. In addition, it outlines a blueprint to strengthen the fight against these crimes.

As part of the overall strategy, the U.S. Marshals Service launched a nationwide operation targeting the top 500 most dangerous, noncompliant sex offenders in the nation. DOJ has laid out goals to increase coordination among the nation's investigators, better train investigators and prosecutors, advance law enforcement's technological capabilities, and enhance research to inform decisions on deterrence, incarceration, and monitoring. The strategy also includes a renewed commitment to public awareness and community outreach. As part of its public outreach efforts, the department relaunched ProjectSafeChildhood.gov, Project Safe Childhood's Web site.

Internet Crimes Against Children Program

The ICAC program is a national network of 61 coordinated task forces representing nearly 3,000 federal, state, and local law enforcement and prosecutorial agencies. These agencies conduct proactive investigations, forensic examinations, and prosecutions. By helping state and local law enforcement agencies develop effective and sustainable responses to online child victimization and child pornography, OJJDP and the ICAC program have built capacity at the local level to address related offenses.

Since the ICAC program's inception in 1998, nearly 286,850 law enforcement officers, prosecutors, and other professionals have been trained throughout the United States and in 17 countries on techniques to investigate and effectively prosecute ICAC-related cases. In addition, the ICAC task forces have reviewed more than 230,300 complaints of alleged child sexual victimization, resulting in the arrest of more than 23,640 individuals

A major source of reports reviewed by ICAC task forces is the National Center for Missing & Exploited Children's (NCMEC's) CyberTipline, which handles phone calls and online reports of sexual exploitation of children. The Cyber-Tipline has received more than 861,000 reports since the system was activated in 1998.

In FY 2010, OJJDP awarded nearly $30 million to support the ICAC task forces, training and technical assistance for the task forces, and research on the scope and consequences of child exploitation. As of August 2010, ICAC task forces had arrested nearly 4,445 individuals, with more than one-third of those arrests (1,733) resulting in the defendant's acceptance of a plea agreement in lieu of a trial.

ICAC task forces received 22,627 reports of technology-facilitated child sexual exploitation from the public and from electronic service providers in FY 2010. Investigations initiated from these reports led to 5,307 arrests, forensics examinations of more than 33,191 computers, and 7,774 case referrals to other law enforcement agencies.

Funded through cooperative agreements, the ICAC Training and Technical Assistance Program provides training for ICAC task force members as well as affiliated law enforcement agencies, prosecutors, computer forensic examiners, parole/probation officers, and judges. In FY 2010, the ICAC program trained approximately 29,733 law enforcement personnel and 2,378 prosecutors.

A highlight of 2010 was the National Internet Crimes Against Children Conference, "PROTECTing our Children: Making the Internet a Safer Place," held in May in Jacksonville, FL. The event is the nation's largest training conference for law enforcement investigators, forensic experts, and prosecutors involved in combating the online exploitation of children. The Acting Deputy Attorney General opened the conference.

The conference featured highly specialized training provided by the ICAC task force program, its federal partner agencies, and other organizations. The conference brought together more than 1,200 federal, state, and local law enforcement investigators, forensic experts, and prosecutors to participate in workshops and lectures on the latest techniques and tools for combating the online exploitation of children.

OJJDP offered more than 140 lecture sessions and more than 70 interactive computer workshops. Training partners included DOJ, U.S. Immigration and Customs Enforcement, the U.S. Marshals Service, the ICAC task force program, the National White Collar Crime Center, the National Center for Justice and the Rule of Law, Girls' Educational and Mentoring Services, the National District Attorneys Association, the Innocent Justice Foundation, SEARCH, and the University of New Hampshire's Crimes against Children Research Center.

Commercial Sexual Exploitation of Children

The commercial sexual exploitation of children (CSEC) involves crimes of a sexual nature committed against juvenile victims for financial or other economic reasons. These crimes include trafficking for sexual purposes, prostitution, sex tourism, mail-order-bride trade and early marriage, pornography, stripping, and performing in sexual venues such as peep shows or clubs. CSEC is not only illegal, it brings about significant and, at times, life-threatening physical, mental, and emotional harm to the victimized youth.

In FY 2010, OJJDP supported a new initiative to help selected law enforcement agencies develop strategies to protect children from commercial sexual exploitation. Areas of focus include improving training and coordination activities, creating policies and procedures to identify victims, investigating and prosecuting cases against adults who sexually exploit children for commercial purposes, and adopting best practices to intervene appropriately with and compassionately serve victims. Agencies receiving funds included the Cook County (IL) State's Attorney's Office, the Georgia Bureau of Investigation, the Boston (MA) Police Department, and the Alameda County (CA) District Attorney's Office.

During FY 2010, much progress was made in OJJDP's Improving Community Response to CSEC initiative, launched in FY 2009 with grants of $500,000 to three communities to strengthen effective collaborations between stakeholder organizations and, ultimately, enhance the effectiveness of community response. During the first year of operation, each of the communities realized significant success in training professionals on the issues of CSEC and in identifying and providing services to victims.

OJJDP PROMOTES PREVENTION OF CHILD ABUSE AT NATIONAL AND INTERNATIONAL CONFERENCES

During FY 2010, OJJDP supported numerous national conferences on the topic of child abuse prevention. In addition to assisting with funding and organization of the events, the Office offered overviews of OJJDP's efforts to protect children and shared strategies for preventing and reducing child maltreatment and children's exposure to violence.

- The 26th National Symposium on Child Abuse, organized by the National Children's Advocacy Center (NCAC) with the support of OJJDP and other sponsors, offered more than 130 training workshops at the Von Braun Center in Huntsville, AL, in March 2010. Each year, OJJDP financially supports the NCAC conference and coordinates the cooperation and participation of other OJJDP grantees at the symposium, including the ICAC task force program, the AMBER Alert program, the Child Protection Division of Fox Valley Technical College, and many others. OJJDP staff presented at numerous workshops, sharing information about OJJDP resources and critical issues in the nationwide effort to combat child abuse.

- The American Professional Society on the Abuse of Children held its 18th Annual Colloquium in New Orleans, LA, in June 2010. The event offered 95 workshops that addressed all aspects of child maltreatment, including prevention, assessment, intervention, and treatment. OJJDP provided workshops on a wide range of topics, including interviewing children about domestic violence, the identification of child mortality due to maltreatment, child forensic interviews, the use of the Internet by child molesters to sexually exploit children, and preparing to defend child interviews in court.

- The 11th Annual Conference on Child Sexual Abuse and Exploitation Prevention took place in New Orleans, LA, in August 2010. Organized by NCAC, the event included workshops on early childhood sexuality and abuse prevention; sexual revictimization in children; school-based intervention programs; sexting, bullying, and online peer harassment; how child abuse impacts Latino families; and community education to protect against child abuse and exploitation, among other subjects.

- The Interagency Children's Policy Council of Alameda County (CA) is supporting the work of the Sexually Exploited Minors Network, a collaboration between the county's public and private providers. The program is offering comprehensive training and education to increase awareness about and promote effective responses to CSEC in the community and has trained nearly 600 professionals in conducting street outreach and strategies to identify and connect high-risk youth to shelter and essential services. This training effort has led to contact with more than 560 youth, the provision of case management services to 29 victims, and emergency shelter care for children in crisis.

- Kristi House, Inc., a Children's Advocacy Center (CAC), is addressing the problem of CSEC in Miami-Dade County, FL, and will expand the project to other Florida cities in partnership with the Florida Department of Children and Families and other CACs in the state. The project will work through the Kristi House-led CSEC Working Group, which consists of 35 agencies. Since receiving funds, Kristi House has trained 295 professionals and is developing a systemwide protocol and set of best practices for addressing the needs of CSEC victims.

- Multnomah County, OR, is using its OJJDP grant to improve local capacity to address CSEC and build on current collaborative efforts. Project staff have trained more than 700 individuals from at least 50 local agencies using a framework supplied by OJJDP and have identified nearly 60 CSEC victims through community partners. Multnomah County will continue to increase the availability of essential services for CSEC victims, including advocacy, emergency housing, mental and physical health services, and the investigation and prosecution of perpetrators of CSEC. It also will continue to promote collaboration between Multnomah County partners to assess local needs and provide interventions.

In July 2010, OJJDP released *Effects of Federal Legislation on the Commercial Sexual Exploitation of Children.* The bulletin examines the effects of the Trafficking and Violence Prevention Act of 2000 on the prosecution of CSEC cases. It discusses how current laws addressing CSEC are enforced, provides the key features of successful CSEC prosecutions, and describes how the juvenile justice community could improve prosecution.

OJJDP ADDRESSES SEXUAL VICTIMIZATION OF CHILDREN BY OTHER YOUTH

Research indicates that youth commit more than one-quarter of all sex offenses and more than one-third of sex offenses against juvenile victims. Additional research on youth who sexually offended against children found that as many as 40 percent of the victims were either siblings or other relatives.

In FY 2010, OJJDP awarded funding to pilot programs in Nebraska, New Jersey, and California to provide comprehensive community-based interventions to serve youth who are identified as having sexual behavior problems and who are in pre- or postadjudication for inappropriate sexual behavior with a family member, co-resident, or other child with close social ties to the perpetrator. Research suggests that by providing intervention services early to youth exhibiting inappropriate sexual behaviors, the likelihood of future incidents and/or escalation is greatly reduced. The funding also supports the development, design, and delivery of technical assistance that provides support and guidance to the sites as they implement their community-based strategies. The University of Oklahoma Health Sciences Center is the technical assistance provider.

In December 2009, OJJDP released the bulletin, *Juveniles Who Commit Sex Offenses Against Minors*, which presents epidemiological information about the characteristics of this population of juvenile offenders. It is hoped that these comprehensive statistical findings will support the development of research-based interventions and policies to reduce the incidence of these serious offenses.

National Center for Missing & Exploited Children

The OJJDP-supported National Center for Missing & Exploited Children observed its 26th year of operation in June 2010. As a clearinghouse and resource center, NCMEC collects and distributes data regarding missing and exploited children. In partnership with OJJDP, the center has offered critical intervention and prevention services to families and has supported law enforcement agencies at the federal, state, and local levels in cases involving missing and exploited children. OJJDP funding for NCMEC totaled approximately $30.5 million in FY 2010.

NCMEC operates a 24-hour, toll-free missing children's hotline (1–800–THE–LOST); a CyberTipline for the public to use to report Internet-related child sexual exploitation; and the Child Victim Identification Program (CVIP), which uses specialized computer software to determine the identities of children whose images appear in pornography.

In FY 2010, the Center's hotline received 104,934 calls. During the same period, its CyberTipline handled 215,840 reports regarding potential child exploitation or online harm to children. As of September 2010, a total of 3,142 identified children were in the CVIP system. During FY 2010, NCMEC assisted in the recovery of 12,060 children; since its inception, NCMEC has assisted in the recovery of 157,722 children.

NCMEC also is a key participant in the annual National Missing Children's Day commemoration and the AMBER Alert program, both described below.

MISSING CHILDREN'S DAY

In 1983, President Reagan proclaimed May 25 as National Missing Children's Day. Since then, citizens, public agencies, and private organizations have gathered in communities across the country to commemorate the day by renewing their commitment to find missing children and celebrating stories of recovery.

In May 2010, the U.S. Department of Justice (DOJ) held its annual commemoration of National Missing Children's Day at DOJ's Great Hall in Washington, DC. Among the dignitaries who spoke at the event were Attorney General Eric Holder and Laurie Robinson, then-Assistant Attorney General for the Office of Justice Programs. Guests included families of missing children; leaders of child advocacy organizations; and federal, state, local, and tribal agency representatives who have supported programs to locate and recover missing children. OJJDP's Acting Administrator presented awards to recognize the outstanding efforts of law enforcement personnel and private citizens who have made a difference in recovering abducted children and protecting children from exploitation. Information about OJJDP publications released at the 2010 Missing Children's Day ceremony is available in chapter 5.

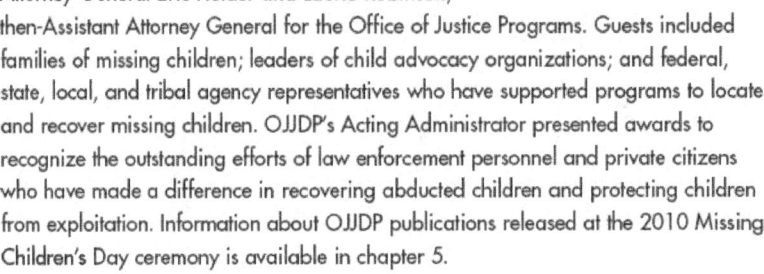

Bringing Our Missing Children Home Safely

AMBER Alert

Launched in 1996, the AMBER Alert program is a voluntary partnership between law enforcement agencies, broadcasters, transportation agencies, and the wireless industry to activate an urgent bulletin in the most serious child abduction cases. The AMBER Alert system issues media alerts on radio, television, highway signs, wireless devices such as mobile phones, and over the Internet when a law enforcement agency determines that a child has been abducted and is in imminent danger. The broadcasts provide information about the child and the abductor that can lead to the child's recovery, such as a physical description of each and a description of the abductor's vehicle. The goal of an AMBER Alert is to instantly galvanize the entire community to assist in the search for and the safe recovery of the child. The Office of Justice Programs (OJP) manages the program with the support of OJJDP. In FY 2010, OJP awarded $3.5 million for the program.

As of September 2010, the AMBER Alert program had helped recover 518 abducted children nationwide. All 50 states, the District of Columbia, Puerto Rico, the U.S. Virgin Islands, and Canada have AMBER Alert plans. AMBER Alert activities include annual national training conferences and local and regional training sessions on topics such as Child Abduction Response Teams (CARTs) and investigative techniques.

Southern Border Initiative

Efforts continue to bring the AMBER Alert program into Mexico through the AMBER Alert Southern Border Initiative. The initiative aims to improve communication and collaboration between U.S. and Mexican law enforcement officials, prosecutors, and child protection professionals and to enhance public participation and notification in cases of child abduction. An advisory team composed of representatives from U.S. and Mexican law enforcement agencies, courts, tribal agencies, social service agencies, child protection organizations, and broadcast media is providing guidance for this project and is assisting in the development of Southern Border Initiative trainings.

The problem of cross-border abduction has reached alarming proportions. According to NCMEC, Mexico is the destination for 47 percent of all international child abductions from the United States. OJJDP is addressing this problem through focused discussions, comprehensive training, and technical assistance.

In 2009, Baja California and Tamaulipas became the first states in Mexico to join the AMBER Alert network. In 2010, the state of Nuevo Leon passed legislation to adopt the AMBER Alert program, and OJJDP staff met with state officials to provide training and technical assistance to support their efforts. In addition, Tamaulipas will provide peer-to-peer technical assistance to Nuevo Leon.

OJJDP held bilingual trainings in San Diego, CA; Brownsville, TX; El Paso, TX; Albuquerque, NM; and Phoenix, AZ, in 2010. The trainings covered a range of topics, including the reporting of missing children, effective strategies for responding to reports, human trafficking, investigative methods, and resources available to address cross-border child abductions. Law enforcement, public safety, and child protection professionals from the United States and Mexico received joint training on the issues and challenges associated with these types of abductions. Simultaneous translation and written materials in English and Spanish were provided. This bilingual effort is critical to child recovery efforts in the border region.

AMBER Alert in Indian Country

Through the AMBER Alert in Indian Country initiative, OJP initially developed AMBER Alert plans in 13 pilot tribal communities. Through the expansion of the AMBER Alert in Indian Country initiative, OJP provided training and technical assistance to additional tribes; currently, 15 tribes have formal AMBER Alert plans and 17 additional tribes are at various levels of development and implementation of their AMBER Alert programs. Assessments of capabilities have been conducted at all sites, with the focus on building capacity within each community to respond to and investigate reports of endangered, missing, or abducted children. OJJDP provided a range of training and technical assistance in FY 2010 to build on these capabilities.

Thirty-two sites have adopted or are in the process of adopting AMBER Alert programs, either alone or in cooperation with state and local authorities, and 15 tribes have passed tribal resolutions or ordinances adopting the AMBER Alert program. All of the participating tribal communities are developing their own CARTs or are participating with local agencies that have CART programs.

In FY 2010, more than 400 tribal community members, government leaders, first responders, child protection officials, and law enforcement officials attended training and technical assistance programs to improve skills and capacity related to a wide range of child protection needs.

Through its Child Protection Programs in Tribal Communities initiative, OJJDP awarded $850,000 in FY 2010 to expand critical services, best practices, tools, and other resources of the AMBER Alert and ICAC programs to protect children in tribal communities who are at risk of exploitation.

NATIONAL SYMPOSIUM ON CHILD PROTECTION IN INDIAN COUNTRY

In March 2010, OJJDP sponsored its first National Symposium on Child Protection in Indian Country in Santa Ana Pueblo, NM. Approximately 280 tribal leaders, law enforcement officials, and representatives of social service agencies from more than 60 tribes participated. OJJDP funded the symposium through the AMBER Alert National Training and Technical Assistance Program and the AMBER Alert in Indian Country initiative.

Larry J. Echo Hawk, the U.S. Department of the Interior's Assistant Secretary for Indian Affairs, delivered remarks on the first day of the symposium. Workshops were designed to foster a multidisciplinary approach and coordinated tribal-based efforts to combat child abuse, neglect, and exploitation in Indian country.

Children's Advocacy Centers

Children's Advocacy Centers (CACs) help coordinate the investigation, treatment, and prosecution of child abuse cases. Recognizing that child abuse is a multifaceted problem, CACs involve multidisciplinary teams of professionals—child protective and victim advocacy services, medical and mental health agencies, and law enforcement and prosecution—to provide a continuum of services to victims and nonoffending family members. In 2010, more than 700 CACs in the United States served 259,000 child victims and treated approximately 400,000 children with preventive measures.

OJJDP has long recognized the efficacy of the CAC model and has provided program funding to expand access to CACs and their valuable services through the Victims of Child Abuse Act of 1990. In FY 2010, $22.5 million was appropriated for the program.

The National Children's Alliance (NCA) serves as the national accrediting and membership body for CACs and administers federal grants to develop and improve these advocacy centers. In collaboration with NCA, the National Children's Advocacy Center (NCAC), and four regional CACs—in the Midwest, Northeast, South, and West—OJJDP works in close partnership to encourage communities to establish local CACs and to provide existing centers with training, technical assistance, and other services.

In FY 2010, NCAC undertook several international initiatives to support the development of CACs and the training of professionals to respond to child abuse. NCAC's international efforts in 2010 included onsite presentations and technical assistance for child abuse professionals in Belarus, Brazil, Denmark, the Faroe Islands, Finland, Iceland, Norway, Russia, and Sweden.

Court Appointed Special Advocates Program

The Court Appointed Special Advocates (CASA) program ensures that abused and neglected children receive culturally sensitive, effective, and timely advocacy in dependency court hearings, ultimately resulting in their placement in safe, permanent homes. CASA volunteers have helped more than 2 million abused children since the first program was established in 1977.

Authorized by the Victims of Child Abuse Act of 1990, as amended, OJJDP administers funding to the National CASA Association, which directs that a "court-appointed special advocate shall be available to every victim of child abuse or neglect in the United States that needs such an advocate." OJJDP partners with the National CASA Association to provide funding for state CASA organizations and new program development as well as expansion of CASA programs and training and technical assistance to volunteer advocates, child welfare professionals, attorneys, judges, and social workers.

The National CASA Association also helps state CASA organizations build their capacity to provide services to local programs. The program makes subgrant funds available to local programs to support court-appointed special advocates who provide advocacy for abused and neglected children in the court system. These trained volunteers, also known as guardians *ad litem*, serve as fact finders, monitors, facilitators, and advocates in cases where there are charges of child abuse and neglect in dependency proceedings. The National CASA Association serves as a resource center, providing support and information dissemination services.

OJJDP's FY 2010 funding for the program totaled nearly $15 million, of which nearly $11 million supported state and local programs and almost $4 million supported training and technical assistance.

Model Courts Program

Studies indicate that children who are abused and neglected are at significantly higher risk for academic failure, chronic delinquency, adult criminal behavior, antisocial personality disorder, and violent crime. In addition, as a child's length of time in out-of-home care increases, the probability of negative outcomes also increases. Preliminary research suggests that more efficient and effective dependency courts can reduce the length of time children spend in the system.

The Model Courts program is a network of juvenile and family courts in 34 states, 1 tribe (the Gila River Indian Community), and the District of Columbia that collaborate to reduce the number of, and achieve better outcomes for, foster children by improving dependency court practice through judicially led system reform. In New York, the Model Courts effort has been implemented as a statewide initiative. The Model Courts program is also establishing important partnerships with tribes to expand Model Courts into additional tribal communities. Developed, managed, and guided by the National Council of Juvenile and Family Court Judges (NCJFCJ) with funding from OJJDP, the project provides tailored training and technical assistance to Model Court jurisdictions and develops cutting-edge national programs and policies.

Each Model Court leads local system reform by selecting short-term improvement goals that are based on proven practices. As a result of the work of the participating courts, programs that have proven to be effective in a single jurisdiction have now become nationwide efforts.

OJJDP supports NCJFCJ's Courts Catalyzing Change: Achieving Equity and Fairness in Foster Care initiative (CCC), a national agenda to reduce the disproportionate representation of and disparate outcomes for children of color in dependency court systems. The program is identifying and evaluating all decision points in the dependency court system and recommending strategies for court and systems change to reduce racial disproportionality and disparate treatment.

The Model Courts program also maintains an active publications program to educate the juvenile justice field on best practices for improving outcomes for children in the dependency court system.

CHAPTER 5

CHAPTER 5

OJJDP Is Providing Resources and Information to the Juvenile Justice Field

The Office of Juvenile Justice and Delinquency Prevention (OJJDP) is a leading and authoritative source of information on juvenile justice issues. The Office disseminates information about its research findings, juvenile justice statistics, and promising programs through comprehensive online databases, Web sites, Webinars, and a wide range of print and online publications.

By sharing the latest research findings on evidence-based programs and practices, OJJDP is playing a central role in the implementation of proven strategies to help prevent and intervene in juvenile delinquency and victimization. The activities discussed in this chapter are ensuring that the juvenile justice field is kept up to date on new developments in research and practice. The Office's efforts in this area help ensure continued progress in the quest to find effective solutions to the juvenile justice field's complex issues and challenges.

OJJDP is keeping the nation informed about critical juvenile justice issues and evidence-based strategies to solve them. The Office's resources include comprehensive online data systems; a Web site featuring the latest information about research, programs, and funding; an online newsletter; and a range of print and online publications.

Sharing Research Findings

The Office recognizes that research findings need to be widely disseminated if they are to be used to improve outcomes for the nation's children. During fiscal year (FY) 2010, the Office shared its research findings with the field through publications as well as at conferences.

Girls Study Group Bulletin Series

As noted in chapter 1, OJJDP convened the Girls Study Group (GSG) in response to the rising arrest rates for girls. Through its research, the GSG aims to gain a better understanding of the dynamics of girls' delinquency and guide policy development regarding female juvenile offenders. OJJDP works closely with the GSG to disseminate the findings from the study group's activities. The Office is currently publishing a series of bulletins highlighting the major findings of the GSG research.

In FY 2010, OJJDP released the fourth and fifth bulletins in the GSG series:

- *Suitability of Assessment Instruments for Delinquent Girls* examines the extent to which existing adolescent assessment instruments used in the juvenile justice system are equally effective for girls and boys.

- *Causes and Correlates of Girls' Delinquency* summarizes the results of the GSG's extensive review of more than 1,600 articles and book chapters from the social science literature on individual-level risk factors for delinquency and factors related to family, peers, school, and communities.

Survey of Youth in Residential Placement Bulletin Series

OJJDP sponsors the nation's most comprehensive data collection program on juvenile offenders in custody and the facilities that hold them. Through a constellation of surveys—which include the Survey of Youth in Residential Placement (SYRP), the Census of Juveniles in Residential Placement (CJRP), and the Juvenile Residential Facility Census (JRFC)—the agency provides critical information to state and national researchers and policymakers who are investigating and seeking answers to major policy and practice questions affecting youth in residential placement, and disseminates those findings to the field. While CJRP and JRFC gather critical data from residential facility administrators, SYRP interviews juveniles directly, providing an unprecedented view of their experiences in custody. Through this approach, SYRP is able to address issues that no other information source covers. For more details on these data collections, see the section "Juveniles in Custody" at the end of this chapter.

To help practitioners, policymakers, and the public better understand youth in custody and the issues facing them, OJJDP has launched a bulletin series that describes SYRP and its findings in detail. The first bulletin in the series, *Introduction to the Survey of Youth in Residential Placement*, reviews SYRP's background and history, describes its design and methodology, discusses its strengths and limitations, and summarizes the questions it answers about the population of youth in custody.

OJJDP'S SAFE START CENTER WINS DESIGN AWARD

In FY 2010, OJJDP's Safe Start Center Web site received a MarCom Gold Award for design. The Web site provides news and resources to practitioners, researchers, and policymakers who work to help children exposed to violence. These children may experience violence as a victim or witness in their home, school, or community. Safe Start online resources include links to recent research, reports, Web sites, training manuals, and best-practice guidelines for practitioners.

Several publications on the site also received MarCom creative awards, including the center's *Issue Brief #2: Pediatric Case Settings*, which received a Platinum Award; and *Issue Brief #1: Understanding Children's Exposure to Violence* and *Healing the Invisible Wounds: Children's Exposure to Violence*, both of which received Gold Awards.

The Safe Start Web site was recently redesigned to meet the latest Web standards and best practices. It displays a rotating banner with the latest news, publications, and research about children exposed to violence. In addition, it allows users to interact with the Safe Start Center through links to social networks such as Twitter, Facebook, and YouTube.

In FY 2010, OJJDP released the second and third bulletins in the series:

- *Youth's Needs and Services* presents key findings on the emotional and psychological problems, substance abuse issues, medical needs, and educational background of youth in residential placement, as well as the services provided by residential facilities to address these issues.

- *Conditions of Confinement* describes the physical features of juvenile facilities, rates the quality of available programs, and reports on access to various social, emotional, and legal supports at the facilities.

National Survey of Children's Exposure to Violence Bulletin Series

As described in detail in chapter 4, OJJDP maintains an active program of research, training, and technical assistance designed to improve the effectiveness of community programs that address the issue of children's exposure to violence. Through his Defending Childhood initiative, the Attorney General has set

DEFENDING CHILDHOOD
PROTECT HEAL THRIVE

this issue as a top priority for the U.S. Department of Justice. A key component of OJJDP's outreach effort is the publication of information based on its research.

In FY 2010, OJJDP launched a National Survey of Children's Exposure to Violence (NatSCEV) bulletin series; the first bulletin in the series, *Children's Exposure to Violence: A Comprehensive National Survey,* was published in October 2009. It summarizes the results of NatSCEV, the most comprehensive study to date on the impact of children's exposure to violence.

The NatSCEV bulletin series will examine a broad range of issues from the survey data, including co-occurrence of family violence, risk factors for exposure to violence in the community, multiple victimizations, and correlates of victimization and mental health. Bulletins will highlight key findings from these various analyses for practitioners, researchers, and policymakers working on behalf of youth and families experiencing or at risk of violence.

PUBLICATIONS FEATURED AT MISSING CHILDREN'S DAY EVENT

At the U.S. Department of Justice's 2010 Missing Children's Day ceremony, OJJDP announced the publication of the fourth edition of *When Your Child Is Missing: A Family Survival Guide.* The guide is one of the resources most widely requested and used by families of missing and abducted children. Among other updates, the publication includes the latest information about new technologies that play a role in facilitating Internet crimes against children.

In addition, OJJDP released *The Crime of Family Abduction: A Child's and Parent's Perspective.* This publication offers unique insight into the emotional and psychological experiences of children during a family abduction and provides parents with helpful advice on assisting their children who are making the transition back to everyday life following their recovery.

OJJDP Web Site

The OJJDP Web site (ojjdp.gov) is a leading online resource for the latest information on a broad range of topics related to juvenile justice. Homepage spotlights feature breaking news on upcoming events and current funding opportunities, as well as publications and other resources. The homepage also provides ready access to the Office's research, publications, programs, and related resources to bring problems such as child abduction, commercial sexual exploitation of children, gang involvement, girls' delinquency, and underage drinking into clearer focus.

The heart of the Web site is its database-driven capability, which gives users quick access to comprehensive information. For example, the Topics page enables users to easily access all items related to specific subject areas, including funding opportunities, programs, events, and publications.

In accordance with OJJDP's commitment to keeping the field informed about the juvenile justice-related activities of other government agencies and organizations, the Web page disseminates timely information about these organizations' meetings, grant opportunities, and publications.

The Web site received approximately 60 million hits in FY 2010; there were approximately 4.6 million visits to the Web site (up from 3.5 million visits in FY 2009) during the same period.

Online Statistical Briefing Book

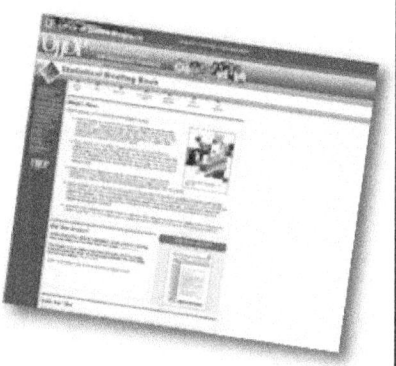

OJJDP has primary responsibility for developing and disseminating statistical information on the juvenile justice system and does so through several mechanisms. OJJDP funds the National Juvenile Court Data Archive, which provides information about cases handled by courts with juvenile jurisdiction. OJJDP established the Archive at the National Center for Juvenile Justice (NCJJ) to provide automated juvenile court data sets. NCJJ produces several annual statistical reports for OJJDP based on Archive data and manages the content for the Statistical Briefing Book (SBB) on OJJDP's Web site.

SBB provides a wealth of information for practitioners, policymakers, the media, and the public. This online tool has current statistics about juvenile crime and victimization and about youth involved in the juvenile justice system. SBB data are continually updated, ensuring that users receive timely and reliable information. SBB has become a primary source of information on juvenile crime and juvenile justice for individuals in the United States and throughout the world. During FY 2010, there were more than 734,000 visits to the SBB site (up from 618,000 in FY 2009) and more than 4 million page views.

I found the information on this Web site to be very useful. The navigation features were timesaving. . . . I would recommend this site to everyone.

—Statistical Briefing Book user

SBB uses Easy Access, a family of Web-based data analysis tools that NCJJ developed for OJJDP to expand access to recent, detailed information on juvenile crime and the juvenile justice system. The Easy Access applications provide information on national, state, and county population counts, as well as information on homicide victims and offenders, juvenile court case processing, and juvenile offenders in residential placement facilities.

FY 2010 updates to SBB included the addition of *Juvenile Court Statistics, 2006–2007*. Developed and produced by NCJJ, the report is one of the nation's oldest justice statistical publications, dating back to 1929. Drawing on data from the National Juvenile Court Data Archive, the most recent report profiles the nearly 1.7 million delinquency cases handled each year by U.S. courts with juvenile jurisdiction in 2006 and 2007. The report also describes trends in delinquency cases processed by juvenile courts between 1985 and 2007 and status offense cases handled between 1995 and 2007.

OJJDP also produced and added four new fact sheets to SBB based on data from the *Juvenile Court Statistics* report: *Delinquency Cases in Juvenile Court, 2007*; *Delinquency Cases Waived to Criminal Court, 2007*; *Juvenile Delinquency Probation Caseload, 2007*; and *Person Offense Cases in Juvenile Court, 2007*. (For more information, see the "Publications" section later in this chapter.)

OJJDP BULLETIN ON JUVENILE TRANSFER LAWS NOW IN PRINT

In FY 2010, OJJDP produced a print version of the bulletin, *Juvenile Transfer Laws: An Effective Deterrent to Delinquency?*, originally released online in 2008. The information provided in the bulletin is helping inform much-needed public discussion and policy decisions on the transfer of juvenile offenders to adult criminal courts.

In August 2008, the publication was highlighted in a *New York Times* editorial underscoring the value of specialized courts for young people. The author of the bulletin cited numerous studies demonstrating higher recidivism rates for juveniles convicted in criminal court than for similar offenders adjudicated in juvenile court.

OJJDP News @ a Glance

OJJDP News @ a Glance highlights major OJJDP activities and priorities, updates from OJJDP-funded programs, new publications, and conferences. This bimonthly newsletter is sent to subscribers via e-mail and is also available on the Web site.

At the end of FY 2010, *News @ a Glance* had more than 28,000 subscribers—reflecting an increase of more than 2,000 subscribers since October 2009.

JUVJUST

OJJDP's electronic listserv, JUVJUST, provides e-mail notices of timely information on juvenile justice and other youth service-related news. JUVJUST subscribers receive brief announcements semiweekly about publications, funding opportunities, conferences, and other valuable resources. JUVJUST reaches more than 20,000 subscribers. JUVJUST announcements are frequently picked up by other governmental and private-sector media, significantly expanding the audience they reach.

To subscribe to *OJJDP News @ a Glance* and JUVJUST, go to the OJJDP Web site, ojjdp.gov (click on the appropriate "Subscribe" button on the homepage). Both services are free.

INFOCUS FACT SHEET SERIES

In FY 2010, OJJDP launched a series of InFocus fact sheets designed to highlight some of the Office's priority activities in an engaging and easy-to-read format. The InFocus fact sheets provide a quick overview of some of OJJDP's major research, programmatic, and training and technical assistance efforts. In 2010, OJJDP won a Communicator Award from the International Academy of the Visual Arts for the fact sheets' design.

Following are the titles of the first six fact sheets, released in FY 2010:

- Community Prevention Grants Program

- Disproportionate Minority Contact

- Enforcing Underage Drinking Laws Program

- Formula Grants Program

- Girls' Delinquency

- Juvenile Accountability Block Grants Program

For more information about these InFocus fact sheets, see the section entitled "Publications."

Publications

OJJDP develops and disseminates a broad range of information about juvenile justice and child protection. The publications described throughout this report play a central role in every facet of OJJDP's mission, from enhancing opportunities for youth to ensuring public safety and supporting law enforcement. Following is a list of the major publications released by OJJDP during FY 2010.

Causes and Correlates of Girls' Delinquency (GSG bulletin). Summarizes the results of the Girls Study Group's extensive review of more than 1,600 articles and book chapters from the social science literature on individual-level risk factors for delinquency and factors related to family, peers, school, and communities. The research team focused on girls ages 11 to 18 and also examined whether these factors are gender neutral, gender specific, or gender sensitive. NCJ 226358.

Children's Exposure to Violence: A Comprehensive National Survey (NatSCEV bulletin). Presents the findings of the National Survey of Children's Exposure to Violence, the first comprehensive attempt in the United States to measure children's exposure to violence in the home, school, and community across all age groups from birth to age 17. The survey is also the first attempt to measure the cumulative exposure to violence over the child's lifetime. NCJ 227744.

Community Prevention Grants Program (InFocus fact sheet). Provides an overview of OJJDP's Community Prevention Grants program, which funds collaborative, community-based delinquency prevention efforts. NCJ 227345.

Conditions of Confinement: Findings From the Survey of Youth in Residential Placement (SYRP bulletin). Presents results from the Survey of Youth in Residential Placement on the characteristics of the facilities in which youth are confined and the programs provided to them. NCJ 227729.

The Crime of Family Abduction: A Child's and Parent's Perspective (report). Helps the reader understand the characteristics of a family abduction and the psychological and emotional impact such criminal activity has on the abducted child and his or her family. NCJ 229933.

Delinquency Cases in Juvenile Court, 2007 (fact sheet). Presents statistics on delinquency cases that U.S. courts with juvenile jurisdiction processed between 1985 and 2007. NCJ 230168.

Delinquency Cases Waived to Criminal Court, 2007 (fact sheet). Presents estimates of the number of cases transferred from juvenile court to criminal court through the judicial waiver mechanism between 1985 and 2007. NCJ 230167.

Disproportionate Minority Contact (InFocus fact sheet). Provides an overview of OJJDP's efforts to reduce the disproportionate number of juvenile members of minority groups who come into contact with the juvenile justice system. NCJ 228306.

Effects of Federal Legislation on the Commercial Sexual Exploitation of Children (bulletin). Presents findings from a study that OJJDP sponsored to examine the effects of the Victims of Trafficking and Violence Prevention Act on the federal prosecution of commercial sexual exploitation of children cases. NCJ 228631.

Enforcing Underage Drinking Laws Program (InFocus fact sheet). Provides an overview of OJJDP's Enforcing Underage Drinking Laws program, which supports and enhances efforts by states and local jurisdictions to reduce the availability of alcohol to minors. NCJ 227469.

Formula Grants Program (InFocus fact sheet). Provides an overview of OJJDP's Formula Grants program, which supports efforts related to delinquency prevention and reduction, juvenile justice system improvement, research, evaluation, statistical analysis, and training and technical assistance. NCJ 227470.

Girls' Delinquency (InFocus fact sheet). Highlights OJJDP's research, programs, publications, and training and technical assistance to address the rising trend in girls' delinquency. NCJ 228414.

Highlights of the 2008 National Youth Gang Survey (InFocus fact sheet). Reports the 2008 findings from the annual survey of U.S. law enforcement agencies. Findings show that an estimated 32.4 percent of all cities, suburban areas, towns, and rural counties experienced gang problems in 2008. NCJ 229249.

Introduction to the Survey of Youth in Residential Placement (SYRP bulletin). Introduces the Survey of Youth in Residential Placement, reviews its background, describes its design and methodology, discusses its strengths and limitations, and summarizes the questions it answers about the population of youth in custody. NCJ 218390.

Juvenile Accountability Block Grants Program (InFocus fact sheet). Provides an overview of OJJDP's Juvenile Accountability Block Grants program, which helps states and communities develop and implement programs that hold youth accountable for delinquent behavior through the imposition of graduated sanctions. NCJ 226357.

Juvenile Arrests 2008 (bulletin). Characterizes the extent and nature of juvenile crime that came to the attention of the justice system in 2008. This bulletin draws on data from the FBI's Uniform Crime Reporting Program, from which the FBI prepares its annual *Crime in the United States* report. NCJ 228479.

Juvenile Court Statistics, 2006–2007 (report). Describes delinquency cases that more than 2,100 U.S. courts with juvenile jurisdiction handled between 1985 and 2007 and petitioned status offense cases handled between 1995 and 2007. NCJ 230105.

Juvenile Delinquency Probation Caseload, 2007 (fact sheet). Presents statistics on delinquency cases resulting in probation between 1985 and 2007. NCJ 230170.

Juvenile Residential Facility Census, 2006: Selected Findings (National Report bulletin). Presents information about the facilities in which juvenile offenders are held, including characteristics such as size, structure, type, ownership, and security arrangements. NCJ 228128.

Juveniles in Residential Placement: 1997–2008 (fact sheet). Examines the changing trends regarding juvenile offenders in residential placement in publicly and privately operated juvenile facilities. NCJ 229379.

Juvenile Transfer Laws: An Effective Deterrent to Delinquency? (bulletin). Provides an overview of research on the effects of transferring juveniles to an adult criminal court, focusing on two large-scale, comprehensive OJJDP-funded studies on the impact of transfer laws on recidivism. NCJ 220595.

Juveniles Who Commit Sex Offenses Against Minors (bulletin). Draws on data from the FBI's National Incident-Based Reporting System to examine the characteristics of youth who commit sexual offenses against minors and their offenses. NCJ 227763.

Person Offense Cases in Juvenile Court, 2007 (fact sheet). Presents statistics on person offense cases that juvenile courts handled between 1985 and 2007. NCJ 230169.

Suitability of Assessment Instruments for Delinquent Girls (GSG bulletin). Examines the extent to which existing adolescent assessment instruments used in the juvenile justice system are equally effective for girls and boys. NCJ 226531.

When Your Child Is Missing: A Family Survival Guide, Fourth Edition (report). Revised from 1998, 2002, and 2004, this report provides parents with the most current information on, and helpful insights into, what families should do when their child is missing. NCJ 228735.

Youth's Needs and Services: Findings From the Survey of Youth in Residential Placement (SYRP bulletin). Presents findings from the Survey of Youth in Residential Placement on how facilities have addressed youth's needs, what services youth receive, and where these services could be improved. NCJ 227728.

All OJJDP publications can be viewed and downloaded from the OJJDP Web site, ojjdp.gov (select the "Publications" section). Print publications can also be ordered online at the National Criminal Justice Reference Service (NCJRS) Web site, ncjrs.gov (select the "A–Z Publications/Products" section). The NCJ numbers at the end of the entries in the above publications list can be used to search for or order resources from NCJRS or to locate specific resources in the NCJRS library, including items produced by OJJDP.

JUVENILES IN CUSTODY

Since OJJDP's inception, an important part of its information dissemination role has been to gather and report data on youth held in public and private juvenile residential placement facilities. As noted earlier in this chapter, the Census of Juveniles in Residential Placement (CJRP) and the Juvenile Residential Facility Census (JRFC), administered by OJJDP in alternate years, provide comprehensive data on juveniles in custody and the facilities that house them. In addition, the Survey of Youth in Residential Placement asks youth about their background and experiences in custody.

Facilities included in both the CJRP and JRFC data collections represent a wide range of facility types: secure and nonsecure, as well as publicly operated (state and local) and privately operated (including long-term and short-term holding). Juvenile facilities go by many different names across the country: detention centers, juvenile halls, shelters, reception and diagnostic centers, group homes, wilderness camps, ranches, farms, youth development centers, residential treatment centers, training or reform schools, and juvenile correctional institutions. Some look like adult prisons or jails, some look like campuses, and others look like houses. This section highlights key findings from the 2010 CJRP and 2008 JRFC and briefly summarizes information on deaths of juveniles in custody from the 2008 JRFC.

Census of Juveniles in Residential Placement 2010

The CJRP provides a 1-day "snapshot" of youth held in public and private juvenile detention and correctional facilities; it includes offense, gender, race, age, and other data. The following highlights are primarily from the census conducted on February 24, 2010.

Overview

* A total of 70,792 youth were held in publicly and privately operated juvenile residential facilities on the 2010 census date. The number of juvenile offenders in residential placement has declined steadily since 2000. The 2000 JRFC registered the largest population of juvenile offenders in residential placement since the data collection expanded in 1974 to include private facilities. In 2010, there were fewer than 71,000 juvenile offenders housed in residential placement—a decline of 35 percent since the peak in 2000 and a 13-percent drop from 2008. The last time that so few juvenile offenders were counted in the national census of juvenile facilities was in 1989, when the tally was slightly less than 67,000.

* Of all juveniles in residential placement, 69 percent were held in public facilities and 31 percent were in private facilities. In addition, tribal facilities reported 177 youth held, Puerto Rico reported 588 youth held, and the U.S. Virgin Islands reported 21 youth held.

- Nearly 7 of 10 juvenile offenders in residential placement had been adjudicated and committed to the facility by the court. Almost 3 of 10 were detained in a facility waiting for their case to be completed or awaiting placement elsewhere.

- Thirty-seven percent of youth in residential placement were there because they were charged with or adjudicated for a person offense. Twenty-four percent were held for a property offense, 16 percent for technical violations of probation or parole, 11 percent for public order offenses, 7 percent for drug offenses, and 4 percent for status offenses. The most common delinquent offenses were technical violations of probation, parole, or valid court order; burglary; robbery; and assault. The most common status offense was ungovernability.

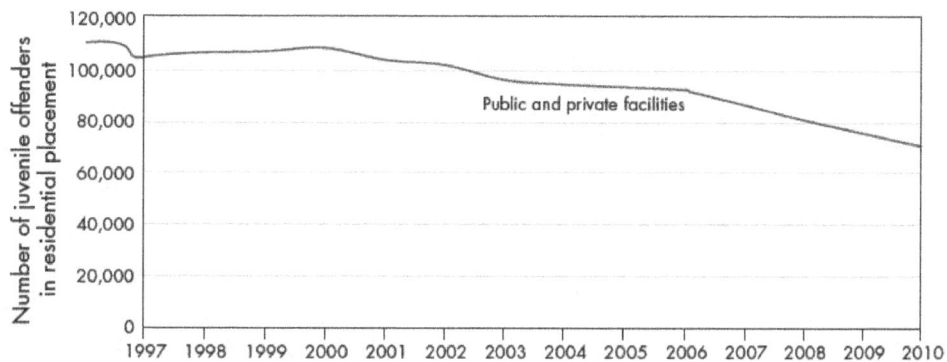

Gender and Age

- Males dominate the juvenile residential placement population. The ratio of males to females is more than six to one.

- More than 9,400 female juvenile offenders were in residential placement on the 2010 census date. The female proportion was 13 percent of offenders in public facilities and 14 percent of offenders in private facilities.

- The offense profiles of males and females were similar in some ways and different in others. For both males and females, drug offenders were less than 10 percent, and drug trafficking offenders were outnumbered by other types of drug offenders. Criminal homicide accounted for only 1 percent of each group. However, for males, aggravated assault offenders outnumbered simple assault offenders. For females, the reverse was true. Among females, 22 percent were held for technical violations of probation, parole, or valid court order. Among males, the proportion was 16 percent. Similarly, status offenders accounted for 11 percent of all females in residential placement, but for only 3 percent of males.

- A greater proportion of female than male juvenile offenders in residential placement were younger than age 16. In 2010, juveniles age 15 or younger accounted for 38 percent of females in custody, compared with 29 percent of males.

Juvenile offenders in residential placement facilities, by age and gender, 2010

	Number			Percent		
	Total	Male	Female	Total	Male	Female
Total	70,792	61,358	9,434	100%	100%	100%
12 or younger	693	559	134	1	1	1
13	2,079	1,711	368	3	3	4
14	5,955	4,905	1,050	8	8	11
15	12,604	10,596	2,008	18	17	21
16	19,540	16,799	2,741	28	27	29
17	19,990	17,608	2,382	28	29	25
18 or older	9,931	9,180	751	14	15	8

Note: Percents may not add to total because of rounding.

Juvenile offenders in residential placement facilities, by most serious offense and gender, 2010

	Number				Percent		
	Total	Male	Female		Total	Male	Female
Total	70,792	61,358	9,434		100%	100%	100%
Delinquency	67,776	59,413	8,363		96	97	89
Criminal homicide	924	837	87		1	1	1
Sexual assault	4,638	4,568	70		7	7	1
Robbery	6,996	6,576	420		10	11	4
Aggravated assault	6,097	5,298	799		9	9	8
Simple assault	5,445	4,134	1,311		8	7	14
Other person	1,910	1,548	362		3	3	4
Burglary	7,247	6,892	355		10	11	4
Theft	3,759	3,074	685		5	5	7
Auto theft	2,469	2,150	319		3	4	3
Arson	533	466	67		1	1	1
Other property	3,029	2,676	353		4	4	4
Drug trafficking	1,034	964	70		1	2	1
Other drug	3,952	3,381	571		6	6	6
Weapons	3,013	2,899	114		4	5	1
Other public order	5,126	4,393	733		7	7	8
Technical violation	11,604	9,557	2,047		16	16	22
Status offense	3,016	1,945	1,071		4	3	11
Curfew	65	52	13		0	0	0
Ungovernable	1,080	683	397		2	1	4
Running away	535	256	279		1	0	3
Truancy	643	442	201		1	1	2
Alcohol	402	289	113		1	0	1
Other status offense	291	223	68		0	0	1

Note: Percents may not add to total because of rounding.

Race/Ethnicity

- Nearly 48,000 minority youth were in residential placement on the 2010 census date, representing 68 percent of all offenders held. Non-Hispanic black youth accounted for 41 percent of the population.

- The overall juvenile residential placement population decreased 32 percent between 2001 and 2010. The decline for white youth was 44 percent, a substantially greater relative decline than the decline among minority youth (24 percent).

- The only group with an increase was the group of youth identified as belonging to two or more non-Hispanic race groups. The increase for this group may have more to do with changes to race identification in the data collection than changes in the numbers of such youth held.

State Data

- Four states—California, Florida, Pennsylvania, and Texas—held 36 percent of the juvenile offenders in residential placement on the census date in 2010. California had the largest population of juvenile offenders in residential placement, with more than 11,500 in placement. Vermont had the smallest residential placement population, with only 33 juvenile offenders in placement.

Juvenile offenders in residential placement facilities, by race/ethnicity

Race/ethnicity	2010 total	Percent	Percent change, 2001–2010
Total	70,792	100%	–32%
Non-Hispanic			
White	22,947	32	–44
Black	28,976	41	–29
American Indian	1,236	2	–39
Asian	516	1	–57
Pacific Islander	212	0	–33
Mixed race	1,315	2	112
Hispanic	15,590	22	–13
Minority	47,845	68	–24

Note: Minority includes all but non-Hispanic white youth.

Juvenile offenders in residential placement facilities, by facility operation, 2010

State of offense	Total	Public	Private	State of offense	Total	Public	Private
U.S. total	70,792	49,112	21,680	Nebraska	750	408	342
Alabama	1,101	561	543	Nevada	717	675	42
Alaska	282	228	54	New Hampshire	117	60	57
Arizona	1,092	969	126	New Jersey	1,179	1,140	39
Arkansas	729	270	459	New Mexico	576	471	105
California	11,532	10,485	1,047	New York	2,637	1,185	1,452
Colorado	1,530	930	600	North Carolina	849	600	249
Connecticut	315	177	138	North Dakota	168	78	90
Delaware	252	201	51	Ohio	2,865	2,661	204
District of Columbia	180	117	66	Oklahoma	639	474	165
Florida	4,815	1,716	3,099	Oregon	1,251	1,020	231
Georgia	2,133	1,728	405	Pennsylvania	4,134	1,008	3,126
Hawaii	120	114	9	Rhode Island	249	99	150
Idaho	480	435	45	South Carolina	984	663	321
Illinois	2,217	1,974	243	South Dakota	504	246	255
Indiana	2,010	1,392	615	Tennessee	789	624	168
Iowa	738	234	501	Texas	5,352	4,902	453
Kansas	843	648	195	Utah	684	378	309
Kentucky	852	768	84	Vermont	33	15	18
Louisiana	1,035	756	282	Virginia	1,860	1,851	9
Maine	186	180	6	Washington	1,305	1,275	30
Maryland	888	681	207	West Virginia	561	348	213
Massachusetts	663	285	378	Wisconsin	1,110	678	432
Michigan	1,998	1,074	924	Wyoming	255	108	150
Minnesota	912	606	306	Tribal	177		
Mississippi	357	318	39	Puerto Rico	588		
Missouri	1,197	1,161	39	Virgin Islands	21		
Montana	192	144	48				

Notes: To preserve the privacy of the juvenile residents, state-level cell counts have been rounded to the nearest multiple of three. "State of offense" refers to the state where the juvenile committed the offense for which he or she was being held. U.S. total includes 2,567 in private facilities for whom state of offense was not reported. U.S. total does not include data reported by tribal and territory facilities.

Juvenile Residential Facility Census 2008

A total of 2,458 facilities reported holding juvenile offenders on the 2008 census date (including 8 tribal facilities). Facilities could identify themselves in more than 1 category: 734 were detention centers, 210 were training schools, 64 were reception/diagnostic centers, 661 were group homes, 847 were residential treatment centers, 85 were ranch/wilderness camps, 167 were shelters, and 31 were boot camps.

A decline in the number of facilities has paralleled the decline in the population of juvenile offenders in residential placement facilities. The decline in facilities has been sharper for privately operated facilities than for publicly operated facilities. Overall, there were 20 percent fewer facilities in 2008 than in 2000. For private facilities, the decrease was 30 percent, and for public facilities it was 4 percent. However, public facilities have accounted for a greater decline in the juvenile offender population: 28 percent from 2000 to 2008 compared with 24 percent for private facilities. In fact, there were nearly three fewer juvenile offenders held in public facilities for every one fewer juvenile in private placement.

These changes have resulted in a reduction in crowding. The proportion of residents that were held in facilities that were at or above the limit of their standard bed capacity decreased 15 percentage points between 2000 and 2008. In 2008, 3 percent of facilities (holding 5 percent of juvenile offenders in residential placement) exceeded their standard bed capacity or had juveniles sleeping in makeshift beds.

In 2008, more than half of facilities were small (20 or fewer residents), although nearly half of juvenile offenders were held in large facilities (more than 100 residents). Small private facilities are the most common type of facility. Private facilities accounted for 53 percent of all facilities, and private facilities with 20 or fewer residents accounted for 66 percent of private facilities. Most of these were group homes. Large facilities were most likely to be state operated. State-operated facilities made up less than one-quarter of all facilities, but they accounted for more than half of facilities holding more than 200 residents.

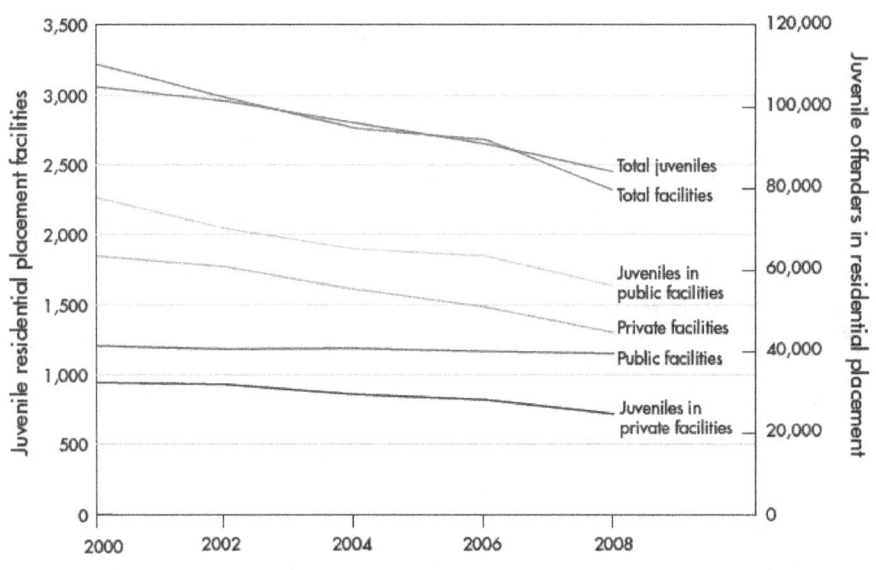

Deaths in Residential Placement

OJJDP's latest data indicate that deaths of juveniles in residential placement remain relatively rare. According to the 2008 JRFC, 14 youth died while in custody at juvenile facilities. Accidents and suicides were the leading causes of death in 2008. There were 5 deaths from accidents (down from 10 in 2006) and 6 deaths by suicide (up from 4 in 2006). There were two deaths from an illness/natural cause and one death from a homicide (by a nonresident outside the facility). The death rate in 2008 (1.7) was substantially lower than the rate in 2000 (2.8). As in previous years, death rates were generally higher in private facilities than in public facilities.

Deaths per 10,000 juveniles held on the census date, October 22, 2008

Type of facility	Total	Public facility	Private facility
Detention center	0.9	1.0	0.0
Training school	2.0	2.1	0.0
Group home	2.6	0.0	4.0
Residential treatment center	1.4	0.0	2.4
Other	2.8	0.0	6.8

Survey of Youth in Residential Placement: Conditions of Confinement

The Survey of Youth in Residential Placement (SYRP) provides answers to a number of questions about the characteristics and experiences of youth in custody, including the conditions under which they are confined. SYRP's findings are based on interviews with a nationally representative sample of 7,073 youth in custody during spring 2003, using audio computer-assisted self-interview methodology.

- Most experts agree that housing young juvenile offenders with older youth should be avoided. Separation of adults and juveniles in custody is also one of the core requirements of the Juvenile Justice and Delinquency Prevention Act. SYRP does not include juveniles who are held in adult prisons and jails, but the findings reveal a considerable age mix in juvenile facilities and substantial mixing of juveniles with young adults.

- One-fifth of offenders in juvenile facilities were in living units with others who are 3 or more years older than they are. Moreover, 43 percent of juveniles in placement were housed in living units with young adults. Such units with older offenders tend to have more serious offenders. Juveniles (younger than age 18) who are in units with young adults are more than twice as likely as juveniles not living in units with young adults (42 percent versus 20 percent) to be living with youth whose most serious career offense is murder.

- Experts recommend housing females in female-only facilities. Thirty-six percent of youth in custody lived in facilities that housed both males and females, and 35 percent of programs were co-ed. However, co-ed placement in living units is uncommon (6 percent). Co-ed placement predominates in detention programs—86 percent of youth were in a co-ed program, and 17 percent were in a co-ed living unit.

- SYRP shows that most youth (63 percent) lived in units where the majority of other residents are person offenders. Nearly one-fifth of the less serious offenders (status offenders, technical parole violators, and youth who report no offense) were placed in living units with youth who have killed someone, and about one-fourth reside with felony sex offenders.

- Unlike serious career offenders for robbery or drug offenders, sex offenders are more typically separated. SYRP indicates that youth who were in custody for a current rape offense were in living units where the majority of residents have rape offense histories (55 percent on average), whereas youth who are in custody for current offenses other than rape were in units where only 6 percent of residents (on average) were felony sex offenders. This type of clustering is dictated to a considerable extent by treatment programs geared toward specific types of offenders. In fact, nearly three-fourths (74 percent) of youth in custody for a current rape offense were in specialized living units for sex offenders.

- SYRP surveyed juvenile offenders only, but administrative data on their facilities also indicate whether they were housed with nonoffenders; 12 percent of youth in residential placement resided in facilities that also housed nonoffenders. Ten percent participated in programs with nonoffenders, and 8 percent resided in primary living units with nonoffenders.

- Several questions focused on issues related to youth's safety in their facilities, including whether they knew what to do in case of fire or how to get help if they were threatened, whether they had ever left their facility without permission, and whether they were afraid of being attacked while living there.

  - Most youth in custody (78 percent) said they know what to do in case of fire in their facility. Only 5 percent reported having left their facility without permission.

  - More than one-third of youth (38 percent) said they feared attack by someone, which includes 25 percent who feared attack by another resident, 22 percent who were afraid that a staff member would physically attack them, and only 15 percent who feared attack by someone coming into the facility from the outside. More females than males expressed a fear of attack from another resident and from someone outside the facility.

  - Ninety percent of youth reported that they knew how to find help if they were threatened or assaulted. More females than males said they feared being attacked (44 percent versus 36 percent)

APPENDIXES

OJJDP Fiscal Year 2010 Awards

In fiscal year (FY) 2010, the Office of Juvenile Justice and Delinquency Prevention (OJJDP) awarded more than $519 million in grants in support of its mission to prevent and respond to juvenile delinquency and child victimization. Of that total, OJJDP awarded $389 million in discretionary grants, which include statutory earmarks and Recovery Act funding.

Formula and Block Grants

Funding through formula and block grants is available to states and territories through the state agency designated by the Governor. Juvenile Justice Specialists in each state administer the funding through subgrants to units of local government, local private agencies, and American Indian/Alaska Native jurisdictions for programs in accordance with legislative requirements. In FY 2010, OJJDP awarded more than $130 million under the following formula and block grants programs:

- Enforcing Underage Drinking Laws Block Grants Program: $19,958,400.

- Juvenile Accountability Block Grants Program: $45,872,293.

- Title II Formula Grants Program: $59,444,862.

- Title V Community Prevention Grants Program: $4,332,246.

Discretionary Grants

OJJDP awards discretionary grants to states, units of local government, and private organizations to administer programs. More than $389 million in discretionary grants was awarded in FY 2010 under the following programs and through statutory earmarks:

- AMBER Alert Training and Technical Assistance Program: $3,150,000.

- Attorney General's Children Exposed to Violence Demonstration Program—Phase I: $1,109,683.

- Child Abuse Training for Judicial and Court Personnel Continuation: $2,473,966.

- Child Protection Division Fellowship Program on Children's Exposure to Violence: $125,000.

- Child Protection Programs in Indian Country: $850,000.

- Community-Based Violence Prevention Demonstration Program: $8,610,392.

- Coordinated Tribal Assistance Solicitation (CTAS) Purpose Area 8—Prevent and Control Delinquency and Improve the Juvenile Justice System (Tribal Youth Program): $9,442,436.

- CTAS Purpose Area 9—Enhance Accountability for Delinquent Behavior (Tribal Juvenile Accountability Discretionary Program): $1,074,686.

- CTAS Purpose Area 10—Develop New Demonstration Projects on Violence Prevention and Rehabilitation (Tribal Youth Program): $3,977,223.

- Court Appointed Special Advocates (CASA) Membership and Accreditation Continuation: $10,960,908.

- CASA Training and Technical Assistance Continuation: $3,882,890.

- Demonstration Programs Division Grants: $12,037,051.

- Enforcing Underage Drinking Laws Assessment, Strategic Planning, and Implementation Initiative: $2,389,625.

- Engaging Law Enforcement Through Training and Technical Assistance To Reduce Juvenile Crime, Victimization, and Delinquency: $749,992.

- Evaluations of Girls' Delinquency Programs: $1,032,156.

- Family Drug Court Programs: $3,046,982.

- Field Initiated Research and Evaluation Program: $1,412,136.

- Group Mentoring Research and Evaluation Program: $1,972,955.

- Internet Crimes Against Children (ICAC) National Training Program—Digital Evidence Forensics: $999,756.

- ICAC National Training Program—Entry Level and Core Training: $1,500,000.

- ICAC National Training Program—Judges Training: $350,000.

- ICAC National Training Program—Officer Wellness: $345,917.

- ICAC National Training Program—Prosecutor Training: $499,995.

- ICAC National Training Program—Specialized Investigative Techniques: $1,836,390.

- ICAC Program—Law Enforcement Strategies for Protecting Children From Commercial Sexual Exploitation: $1,199,999.

- ICAC Program Support: $2,000,000.

- ICAC Task Force Continuation Program: $17,445,553.

- ICAC Task Force—Minnesota: $320,000.

- Juvenile Drug Courts and Mentoring Initiative: $2,952,690.

- Juvenile Drug Courts Program: $1,249,979.

- Juvenile Drug Courts Training and Technical Assistance Program: $1,222,329.

- Juvenile Indigent Defense National Clearinghouse: $500,000.

- Juvenile Workforce Development Programs in El Paso, TX: $99,975.

- Membership Support Services for Nonprofit Missing Children's Organizations Continuation Program: $225,000.

- Mentoring Research Best Practices: $2,716,108.

- Mentoring for Safe Schools/Healthy Students Initiatives: $2,974,465.

- Missing and Exploited Children Program Support: $350,000.

- Missing and Exploited Children National Training Program: $1,890,000.

- Multi-State Mentoring Initiative: $18,000,000.

- National Center for Missing & Exploited Children Program: $29,702,900.

- National Evaluation of the Community-Based Violence Prevention Program: $1,074,992.

- National Evaluation of Safe Start Promising Approaches: $765,216.

- National Girls Institute: $500,000.

- National Incidence Studies of Missing, Abducted, Runaway, and Thrownaway Children 3: $1,000,000.

- National Juvenile Justice Data Analysis Program: $800,000.

- National Juvenile Justice Evaluation Center: $393,160.

- National Mentoring Programs: $60,000,000.

- National Survey on Children Exposed to Violence—New Cohort Continuation: $1,089,872.

- National Training and Technical Assistance Center for Youth in Custody: $500,000.

- Nonparticipating State Program—Wyoming: $570,000.

- Research on Technology-Facilitated Crimes Against Children: $1,763,372.

- Safe Start Promising Approaches Project: $2,497,162.

- Second Chance Act Adult and Juvenile Offender Reentry Demonstration Projects: $7,955,996.

- Second Chance Act Juvenile Mentoring Initiative: $5,018,909.

- State Relations and Assistance Division State Advisory Group Training and Technical Assistance Project: $400,000.

- Strategic Enhancement to Mentoring Programs: $5,605,312.

- Support for Conferences on Juvenile Justice: $80,000.

- Tribal Youth Field Initiated Research and Evaluation Programs: $500,000.

- Tribal Youth National Mentoring Program: $5,199,507.

- Tribal Youth Program Training and Technical Assistance: $3,149,825.

- Victims of Child Abuse (VOCA) Act Children's Advocacy Centers Membership and Accreditation Continuation: $1,132,137.

- VOCA Children's Advocacy Centers Subgrant Continuation: $13,189,317.

- VOCA Regional Children's Advocacy Centers Program: $5,966,827.

- VOCA Training and Technical Assistance for Child Abuse Professionals Continuation: $954,547.

- VOCA Training and Technical Assistance for Child Abuse Prosecutors Continuation: $1,864,696.

- Youth Gang Prevention and Intervention Program: $2,986,884.

- Youth With Sexual Behavior Problems Program: $1,450,000.

Statutory Earmarks

A list of statutory earmark award recipients is available on the OJJDP Web site, ojjdp.gov (click on "Funding").

Recovery Act Awards

Under the American Recovery and Reinvestment Act of 2009, OJJDP awarded discretionary funding for the following initiative in FY 2010:

- Recovery Act—Needs Assessment and Developmental Activities for the National Internet Crimes Against Children Data System (NIDS): $921,000.

Award information for FYs 2007–2011 is available on the OJJDP Web site.

OJJDP APPENDIX B

State Compliance With JJDP Act Core Requirements

T

productive, successful lives. The program also provides funds to enhance the effectiveness of the juvenile justice system.

To receive funding, states must commit to achieving and maintaining compliance with the four core requirements of the Juvenile Justice and Delinquency Prevention (JJDP) Act of 1974, as amended: deinstitutionalization of status offenders, separation of juveniles from adults in secure facilities, removal of juveniles from adult jails and lockups, and reduction of disproportionate minority contact within the juvenile justice system.

If a state, despite its good faith efforts, fails to demonstrate compliance with any of the core requirements in any year, OJJDP will reduce its formula grant for the subsequent fiscal year by 20 percent for each requirement for which the state is noncompliant. The following table indicates (in green) the states that received reduced fiscal year (FY) 2010 funding for noncompliance with one or more of the JJDP Act's core requirements.

FY 2010 Funding Reductions for Noncompliance

State[1]	Deinstitutionalization of status offenders	Separation of juveniles from adults in secure facilities	Removal of juveniles from adult jails and lockups	Reduction of disproportionate minority contact
Alabama	√	√	√	√
Alaska	√	√	√	√
Arizona	√	√	√	√
Arkansas	X	√	X	√
California	√	√	√	√
Colorado	√	√	√	√
Connecticut	√	√	√	√
Delaware	√	√	X	√
District of Columbia	√	√	√	√
Florida	√	√	√	√
Georgia	√	√	√	√
Hawaii	√	√	√	√
Idaho	√	√	√	√
Illinois	√	√	√	√
Indiana	√	√	√	√
Iowa	√	√	√	√
Kansas	√	√	√	√
Kentucky	√	√	√	√
Louisiana	√	√	√	√
Maine	√	√	√	√
Maryland	√	√	√	√
Massachusetts	√	√	√	√
Michigan	√	√	√	√
Minnesota	√	√	√	√
Mississippi	X	√	X	√
Missouri	√	√	√	√
Montana	√	√	√	√
Nebraska	√	√	√	√
Nevada	√	√	√	√
New Hampshire	√	√	√	√
New Jersey	√	√	√	√
New Mexico	√	√	√	√
New York	√	√	√	√
North Carolina	X	X	X	√
North Dakota	√	√	√	√
Ohio	√	√	√	√

State[1]	Deinstitutionalization of status offenders	Separation of juveniles from adults in secure facilities	Removal of juveniles from adult jails and lockups	Reduction of disproportionate minority contact
Oklahoma	√	√	√	√
Oregon	√	√	√	√
Pennsylvania	√	√	√	√
Rhode Island	√	√	√	√
South Carolina	√	√	X	√
South Dakota	√	√	√	√
Tennessee	√	√	√	√
Texas	√	√	√	√
Utah	√	√	√	√
Vermont	√	√	√	√
Virginia	√	√	√	√
Washington	X	√	√	√
West Virginia	√	√	√	√
Wisconsin	√	√	√	√
Wyoming[2]	–	–	–	–
American Samoa	√	√	√	√
Guam	X	X	X	√
Northern Mariana Islands	X	√	√	√
Puerto Rico[3]	√	X	X	–
Virgin Islands	X	X	X	√

X = reduced FY 2010 funding for noncompliance; √ = full FY 2010 funding for compliance.

[1] The term "state" means any state of the United States, the District of Columbia, and the five U.S. territories.

[2] Wyoming does not participate in the Formula Grants program.

[3] The U.S. Census Bureau has exempted Puerto Rico from reporting racial statistics.

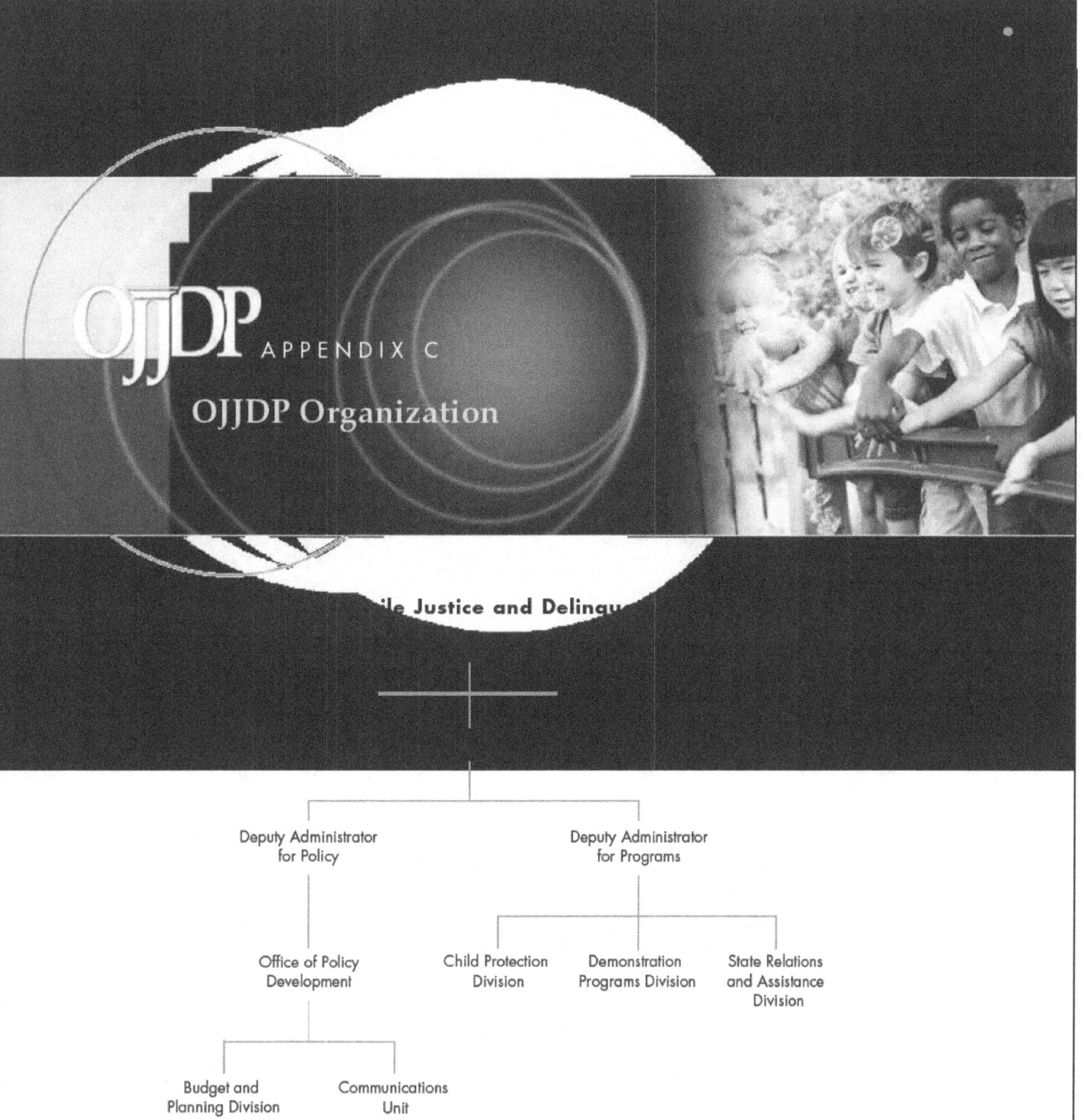

OJJDP

APPENDIX C

OJJDP Organization

...ile Justice and Delinqu...

Deputy Administrator for Policy	Deputy Administrator for Programs

Office of Policy Development	Child Protection Division	Demonstration Programs Division	State Relations and Assistance Division

Budget and Planning Division	Communications Unit

Office of the Administrator

The Office of the Administrator (OA) establishes OJJDP's priorities and policies, oversees the management of the Office's divisions, and fosters collaboration with federal, state, and local agencies and associations that share OJJDP's commitment to preventing and combating juvenile delinquency and addressing the problem of missing and exploited children.

Office of Policy Development

The Office of Policy Development (OPD) assists the OJJDP Administrator in coordinating national policy on juvenile justice. OPD advises the Administrator on policy and legal issues and how OJJDP can best accomplish its mission. OPD also provides leadership and direction for OJJDP's research and training and technical assistance efforts and oversees the agency's communications and planning activities.

Communications Unit

The Communications Unit (CU) is responsible for OJJDP's information dissemination and outreach. CU develops OJJDP publications, manages its Web site and online services, and performs a range of writing and editing functions to support the Office. CU also serves as a liaison to the Office of Justice Programs on media-related issues.

Budget and Planning Division

The Budget and Planning Division handles OJJDP's budget and planning operations and manages the Office's research and training and technical assistance functions. The division also oversees all administrative and personnel matters.

Child Protection Division

The Child Protection Division (CPD) develops and administers programs related to crimes against children and children's exposure to violence. It provides leadership and funding in the areas of enforcement, intervention, and prevention. CPD's activities include supporting programs that promote effective policies and procedures to respond to the problems of missing and exploited children, Internet crimes against children, abused and neglected children, and children exposed to domestic or community violence.

Demonstration Programs Division

The Demonstration Programs Division (DPD) provides funds to public and private agencies, organizations, and individuals to develop and support programs and replicate tested approaches to delinquency prevention, treatment, and control in areas such as mentoring, substance abuse, gangs, truancy, chronic juvenile offending, and community-based sanctions. DPD also supports and coordinates efforts with tribal governments to expand and improve tribal juvenile justice systems and develop programs and policies that address problems facing tribal youth.

State Relations and Assistance Division

The State Relations and Assistance Division (SRAD) provides funds to help state and local governments achieve the system improvement goals of the Juvenile Justice and Delinquency Prevention Act of 1974, as amended; combat underage drinking; implement delinquency prevention programs; address disproportionate minority contact; and support initiatives to hold juvenile offenders accountable for their actions. SRAD also supports and coordinates community efforts to identify and respond to critical juvenile justice and delinquency prevention needs.